THIS BOOK BELONGS TO

The Library of

....

....

I can't tell you how grateful I am that you decided to read my book. My most heartfelt thanks that you took time out of your life to choose my work and I hope you find benefit within these pages.

There are so many books available today that offer similar content so that makes it even more humbling that you decided to buying mine.

Tell me what you thought! I am eager to hear your opinion and ideas on what you read as are others who are looking for a good book to buy. Leave a review on Amazon.com so others can benefit from your wisdom!

With much thanks.

Table of Contents

SUMMARY

Crochet and flower loom crafting have gained immense popularity in recent years, captivating the hearts of many individuals. These crafts possess a unique allure that draws people in and keeps them hooked.

Crochet, a technique of creating fabric using a hooked needle, offers a plethora of possibilities. The process involves interlocking loops of yarn to form intricate patterns and designs. What makes crochet so appealing is its versatility. From delicate doilies to cozy blankets, the possibilities are endless. The ability to create beautiful and functional items with just a hook and some yarn is truly captivating.

One of the main reasons why crochet has become so popular is its therapeutic nature. Many individuals find solace in the rhythmic motion of the hook, which can be incredibly calming and meditative. The repetitive nature of crochet allows the mind to relax and focus solely on the task at hand, providing a much-needed escape from the stresses of everyday life. Additionally, the sense of accomplishment that comes with completing a crochet project can boost one's self-esteem and provide a sense of fulfillment.

Flower loom crafting, on the other hand, offers a different kind of allure. This technique involves using a flower loom tool to create intricate and beautiful flowers. The process is simple yet captivating, as one weaves yarn or thread around the loom's pegs to form petals. The end result is a stunning flower that can be used in various ways, such as embellishments for clothing, accessories, or even home decor.

What makes flower loom crafting so appealing is its accessibility. Unlike other crafts that may require extensive knowledge or expensive equipment, flower loom crafting can be enjoyed by anyone, regardless of their skill level or budget. The tools are affordable and easy to use, making it a great option for beginners or those looking for a new creative outlet.

Furthermore, flower loom crafting allows for endless creativity. With a wide range of yarn colors and textures available, one can create flowers in various sizes and styles. The ability to mix and match different yarns and experiment with different techniques adds an element of excitement and personalization to each project.

Both crochet and flower loom crafting offer a sense of accomplishment and pride in creating something beautiful with one's own hands. The satisfaction of seeing a project come to life, whether it's a cozy scarf or a vibrant flower, is truly rewarding. These crafts also provide a sense of community, as individuals can connect with fellow crafters through online forums, social media groups, or local meetups.

The book provides a comprehensive overview of its content and clearly outlines its objectives. It begins by introducing the reader to the main themes and concepts that will be explored throughout the book. The author takes great care in presenting a detailed overview of the subject matter, ensuring that readers have a solid foundation before delving into more complex topics.

The book's content is organized in a logical and structured manner, allowing readers to easily navigate through the chapters and sections. Each chapter focuses on a specific aspect of the subject, providing in-depth analysis and discussion. The author incorporates a variety of examples, case studies, and real-life scenarios to illustrate key points and enhance understanding.

One of the main objectives of the book is to provide readers with a comprehensive understanding of the subject matter. The author achieves this by presenting information in a clear and concise manner, avoiding unnecessary jargon or technical language. The book is written in a way that is accessible to both experts in the field and those who are new to the subject.

Another objective of the book is to encourage critical thinking and analysis. The author poses thought-provoking questions and challenges readers to consider different perspectives and interpretations. This not only enhances the learning experience but also fosters a deeper understanding of the subject matter.

Furthermore, the book aims to provide practical guidance and tools that readers can apply in real-world situations. The author includes practical tips, strategies, and techniques that can be implemented to achieve desired outcomes. This ensures that readers not only gain theoretical knowledge but also develop practical skills that can be utilized in their personal or professional lives.

Overall, the book's content and objectives are well-defined and thoughtfully presented. It offers a comprehensive overview of the subject matter, encourages critical thinking, and provides practical guidance. Whether you are a student, professional, or simply interested in the topic, this book is a valuable resource that will enhance your understanding and knowledge.

When it comes to any task or project, having the right tools and materials is crucial for success. Whether you are a professional or a DIY enthusiast, having a well-stocked toolbox is essential. Here are some of the most important tools and materials that should be included in your arsenal:

1. Screwdrivers: A set of screwdrivers with different sizes and types of heads is a must-have. They are used for tightening or loosening screws in various applications.

2. Hammer: A good quality hammer is indispensable for any kind of construction or repair work. It is used for driving nails, removing nails, and general pounding tasks.

3. Pliers: Pliers come in various types such as needle-nose, slip-joint, and locking pliers. They are used for gripping, bending, and cutting wires or other materials.

4. Tape measure: Accurate measurements are crucial in any project. A tape measure helps you measure distances, lengths, and widths accurately.

5. Level: A level is used to determine if a surface or object is perfectly horizontal or vertical. It is essential for hanging pictures, shelves, or any other items that need to be level.

6. Utility knife: A utility knife is a versatile tool that can be used for cutting various materials such as cardboard, plastic, or even carpet.

7. Power drill: A power drill is a handy tool that can be used for drilling holes, driving screws, or even mixing paint or cement with the right attachments.

8. Safety equipment: Safety should always be a priority. Safety glasses, gloves, and ear protection are essential tools to protect yourself from potential hazards.

In addition to these tools, there are also various materials that are essential for different projects. Some of the most commonly used materials include:

1. Nails and screws: These fasteners are used to join materials together. They come in different sizes and types, such as wood screws, drywall screws, or finishing nails.

2. Adhesives: Adhesives such as glue, epoxy, or tape are used to bond materials together. They are essential for various applications, from woodworking to crafting.

3. Paint and brushes: If you are planning to paint a room or furniture, having the right paint and brushes is crucial. Different types of paint and brushes are suitable for different surfaces and finishes.

A. Detailed crochet stitch tutorials and practice exercises provide a comprehensive and in-depth learning experience for individuals interested in mastering the art of crochet. These tutorials offer step-by-step instructions, accompanied by clear and concise explanations, ensuring that beginners and experienced crocheters alike can easily follow along.

The tutorials cover a wide range of crochet stitches, from basic stitches such as single crochet and double crochet to more intricate stitches like the shell stitch and popcorn stitch. Each stitch is thoroughly explained, including the number of loops and yarn overs required, as well as the specific movements and techniques involved. This level of detail allows learners to understand the mechanics of each stitch, enabling them to replicate it accurately and consistently.

In addition to the stitch tutorials, the practice exercises provided offer an opportunity for hands-on learning and skill development. These exercises are designed to reinforce the techniques learned in the tutorials and help learners gain confidence in their crochet abilities. They may include projects such as creating a simple scarf or a small amigurumi toy, allowing individuals to apply their newly acquired skills in a practical and enjoyable way.

The detailed nature of these tutorials and exercises ensures that learners have access to all the information they need to succeed in their crochet journey. Whether someone is a visual learner who benefits from detailed images and diagrams or a more text-oriented learner who prefers written instructions, these resources cater to various learning styles. The tutorials often include high-quality photographs or illustrations, providing visual aids that enhance the learning experience and make it easier to understand the intricacies of each stitch.

Furthermore, these tutorials and exercises are designed to be accessible to individuals of all skill levels. Beginners can start with the basics and gradually progress to more advanced stitches, while experienced crocheters can use them as a refresher or to expand their repertoire of stitches. The clear explanations and practice exercises ensure that learners can build a solid foundation and continue to develop their skills at their own pace.

In conclusion, detailed crochet stitch tutorials and practice exercises offer a comprehensive and effective way for individuals to learn and improve their crochet skills. With step-by-step instructions, clear explanations, and practical exercises, these resources provide a thorough understanding of various crochet stitches and techniques. Whether someone is a beginner or an experienced crocheter, these tutorials and exercises cater to different learning styles and skill levels, making them an invaluable tool for anyone interested in mastering the art of crochet.

One way to enhance flower loom projects is by integrating crochet elements into them. Crochet is a versatile and intricate craft that can add depth, texture, and visual interest to any project. By combining the techniques of flower looming and crochet, you can create unique and stunning pieces that stand out from the crowd.

To begin incorporating crochet into your flower loom projects, you will need to have a basic understanding of both crafts. Flower looming involves using a circular loom to create flowers or other circular designs by wrapping yarn around pegs and then weaving it together. Crochet, on the other hand, involves using a hook to create stitches and patterns with yarn.

One way to integrate crochet into flower loom projects is by adding crochet borders or edgings to your loomed flowers. This can be done by crocheting around the outer edge of the flower, adding a decorative and finished look. You can experiment with different crochet stitches and patterns to create unique borders that complement the colors and shapes of your loomed flowers.

Another way to incorporate crochet into flower loom projects is by creating crochet motifs or appliques to attach to your loomed flowers. These can be small crochet designs, such as leaves, petals, or other decorative elements, that are then sewn or glued onto the loomed flowers. This adds an extra layer of dimension and intricacy to your projects, making them truly one-of-a-kind.

Additionally, you can combine flower looming and crochet techniques to create hybrid designs. For example, you can use the flower loom to create the base of a project, such as a hat or a bag, and then use crochet to add embellishments or details. This allows you to take advantage of the unique texture and structure of flower loom projects while also incorporating the versatility and creativity of crochet.

When integrating crochet elements into flower loom projects, it is important to consider the materials and yarns you use. Different yarn weights and textures can create different effects, so experiment with a variety of options to find the perfect combination for your desired outcome. Additionally, consider the color palette and overall aesthetic of your project to ensure that the crochet elements seamlessly blend with the loomed flowers.

In conclusion, integrating crochet elements into flower loom projects can elevate your creations to a whole new level. By combining the techniques of flower looming and crochet, you can create intricate, textured, and visually stunning pieces that are truly unique.

Detailed projects with step-by-step instructions provide a comprehensive and thorough guide for individuals looking to engage in a specific task or activity. These projects offer a wealth of information and guidance, ensuring that users have all the necessary knowledge and resources to successfully complete the project.

The step-by-step instructions included in these detailed projects break down the entire process into manageable and easily understandable steps. This allows users to follow along and progress through the project at their own pace, ensuring that they do not miss any crucial steps or make any mistakes along the way.

One of the key benefits of detailed projects with step-by-step instructions is that they cater to individuals with varying levels of expertise. Whether you are a beginner or an experienced individual, these projects provide the necessary guidance to help you achieve your desired outcome. Beginners can rely on the detailed instructions to learn new skills and techniques, while experienced individuals can use the projects as a reference or source of inspiration to enhance their existing knowledge.

Furthermore, these projects often include detailed materials lists, tools required, and even alternative options or suggestions. This ensures that users have a clear understanding of what they need to complete the project and can make informed decisions about the resources they have available. Additionally, the inclusion of alternative options or suggestions allows users to customize the project to their preferences or adapt it based on the materials and tools they have access to.

Detailed projects with step-by-step instructions also promote a sense of accomplishment and satisfaction. As users progress through each step and see their project come to life, they gain a sense of achievement and pride in their work. This can be particularly rewarding for individuals who enjoy hands-on activities or creative endeavors.

Moreover, these projects can serve as a valuable learning tool. By following the step-by-step instructions, users can gain new skills, expand their knowledge, and develop a deeper understanding of the subject matter. This can be particularly beneficial for individuals looking to pursue a hobby or explore a new area of interest.

In conclusion, detailed projects with step-by-step instructions offer a comprehensive and thorough guide for individuals looking to engage in a specific task or activity. They provide users with the necessary knowledge, resources, and guidance to successfully complete the project, regardless of their level of expertise. These projects promote a sense of accomplishment, serve as a valuable learning tool, and can be customized to suit individual preferences and available resources.

A. Exploring advanced crochet and flower loom techniques

In this workshop, participants will have the opportunity to delve deeper into the world of crochet and flower loom techniques. Whether you are a beginner looking to expand your skills or an experienced crocheter wanting to take your craft to the next level, this workshop is designed to provide you with the knowledge and techniques needed to create intricate and beautiful crochet projects.

Throughout the workshop, you will be introduced to a variety of advanced crochet stitches and techniques, such as filet crochet, Tunisian crochet, and tapestry crochet. These techniques will allow you to create more complex and detailed designs, adding depth and texture to your crochet projects. You will also learn how to read and follow advanced crochet patterns, enabling you to tackle more challenging projects with confidence.

In addition to exploring advanced crochet techniques, this workshop will also introduce you to the art of flower loom weaving. Flower loom weaving is a versatile and creative technique that allows you to create stunning floral designs using yarn and a flower loom tool. You will learn how to create different types of flowers, such as roses, daisies, and sunflowers, and how to incorporate them into your crochet projects.

Throughout the workshop, you will have the opportunity to practice and apply the techniques learned through hands-on projects. You will be guided by an experienced instructor who will provide step-by-step demonstrations and individualized feedback to help you master each technique. By the end of the workshop, you will have completed several advanced crochet projects and flower loom designs, showcasing your newfound skills and creativity.

Whether you are looking to create intricate doilies, beautiful shawls, or unique home decor items, this workshop will equip you with the tools and techniques needed to bring your crochet projects to life. Join us in exploring the world of advanced crochet and flower loom techniques and take your craft to new heights.

If you are a creative individual who loves making handmade accessories, you may be wondering how you can turn your passion into a profitable venture. Whether you want to gift your creations to loved ones or sell them to a wider audience, there are plenty of ideas and strategies you can explore to make the most of your handmade accessories.

When it comes to gifting your handmade accessories, the possibilities are endless. One idea is to create personalized pieces for your friends and family. Consider their individual tastes, preferences, and interests, and design accessories that reflect their unique personalities. For example, if your best friend loves nature, you could make a necklace with a pendant shaped like a leaf or a bracelet adorned with tiny flowers. Personalized accessories not only show that you put thought and effort into the gift, but they also make the recipient feel special and cherished.

Another gifting idea is to create matching sets of accessories for couples, siblings, or best friends. For instance, you could make a pair of earrings for a couple that complement each other, or design bracelets for siblings that have their initials engraved on them. These matching sets not only make for a thoughtful gift, but they also serve as a symbol of the bond between the recipients.

If you want to sell your handmade accessories, there are several avenues you can explore. One option is to set up an online store on platforms such as Etsy or Shopify. These platforms provide a user-friendly interface for you to showcase and sell your products to a global audience. Make sure to take high-quality photographs of your accessories and write detailed descriptions to attract potential buyers. Additionally, consider offering customization options or limited edition pieces to make your products stand out from the competition.

Another selling idea is to participate in local craft fairs or markets. These events provide an opportunity for you to interact with customers directly and receive immediate feedback on your products. Set up an attractive booth that showcases your accessories in an appealing way, and be prepared to answer questions and engage with potential buyers. Consider offering special promotions or discounts during these events to incentivize purchases.

Collaborating with local boutiques or stores is another avenue to explore. Approach small businesses that align with your brand aesthetic and inquire about the possibility of selling your accessories in their stores. This can help you reach a wider customer base and benefit from the store's existing customer traffic. Make sure to establish clear terms and agreements with the store regarding pricing, consignment, or wholesale options.

A. Recommended books, websites, and online communities

When it comes to expanding our knowledge and exploring new ideas, books, websites, and online communities play a crucial role. They provide us with a wealth of information, connect us with like-minded individuals, and offer a platform for learning and growth. In this regard, I would like to recommend some exceptional resources that have personally enriched my life and can potentially do the same for you.

Books have always been a gateway to new worlds and perspectives. They allow us to delve into various subjects, from history and science to philosophy and literature. One book that I highly recommend is Sapiens: A Brief History of Humankind by Yuval Noah Harari. This thought-provoking book takes us on a journey through the history of our species, exploring the key events and developments that have shaped our present reality. It challenges our preconceived notions and encourages us to question the status quo.

Another book that has had a profound impact on me is The Power of Now by Eckhart Tolle. This spiritual guide teaches us the importance of living in the present moment and finding inner peace. It offers practical advice on how to overcome negative thought patterns and embrace a more mindful and fulfilling existence.

In addition to books, websites have become an invaluable source of information in today's digital age. One website that I highly recommend is TED.com. TED Talks feature experts from various fields who share their insights and ideas in engaging and thought-provoking presentations. From science and technology to art and psychology, TED Talks cover a wide range of topics, making it a treasure trove of knowledge and inspiration.

When it comes to online communities, Reddit.com stands out as a platform that brings people together based on shared interests. With thousands of communities, or subreddits, dedicated to specific topics, it offers a space for individuals to connect, discuss, and learn from one another. Whether you're interested in photography, fitness, or personal finance, there is a subreddit for you. The diverse perspectives and experiences shared within these communities can be incredibly valuable in expanding our understanding and broadening our horizons.

In conclusion, books, websites, and online communities are invaluable resources for personal growth and learning. The recommended books, websites, and online communities mentioned above are just a few examples of the vast array of resources available to us.

Reflecting on my journey as a crochet and flower loom artist, I am filled with a sense of accomplishment and growth. It all began several years ago when I stumbled upon the art of crochet and instantly fell in love with the intricate patterns and endless possibilities it offered. Little did I know that this newfound passion would lead me down a path of creativity and self-discovery.

As I delved deeper into the world of crochet, I found myself experimenting with different stitches, techniques, and yarns. Each project became a canvas for me to express my artistic vision and explore the boundaries of my skills. From simple scarves and hats to intricate doilies and blankets, I challenged myself to constantly push the limits of what I could create with a hook and some yarn.

But it wasn't just crochet that captivated me; I soon discovered the art of flower loom weaving. This technique allowed me to create beautiful, delicate flowers using a small loom and colorful threads. The process of weaving each petal and assembling them into a stunning blossom was both meditative and rewarding. It added a new dimension to my artistic repertoire and opened up a whole new world of possibilities.

Throughout my journey, I have encountered numerous challenges and setbacks. There were times when I struggled to master a particular stitch or when a project didn't turn out as planned. However, these obstacles only fueled my determination to improve and learn from my mistakes. With each setback, I grew more resilient and developed a deeper understanding of the craft.

One of the most rewarding aspects of being a crochet and flower loom artist is the joy and satisfaction I derive from seeing my creations come to life. Whether it's a cozy blanket that brings comfort to someone on a cold winter night or a vibrant bouquet of flowers that brightens up a room, the impact of my art on others is truly fulfilling. It is a reminder of the power of creativity to touch hearts and evoke emotions.

Moreover, my journey as an artist has also allowed me to connect with a vibrant and supportive community of fellow crochet and flower loom enthusiasts. Through online forums, workshops, and local meetups, I have

Flower Loom Instructions

Basic Instructions

1. Select loom shape and set shape on the base, lining the notches on the bottom of the loom to the opposite indentations on the base.

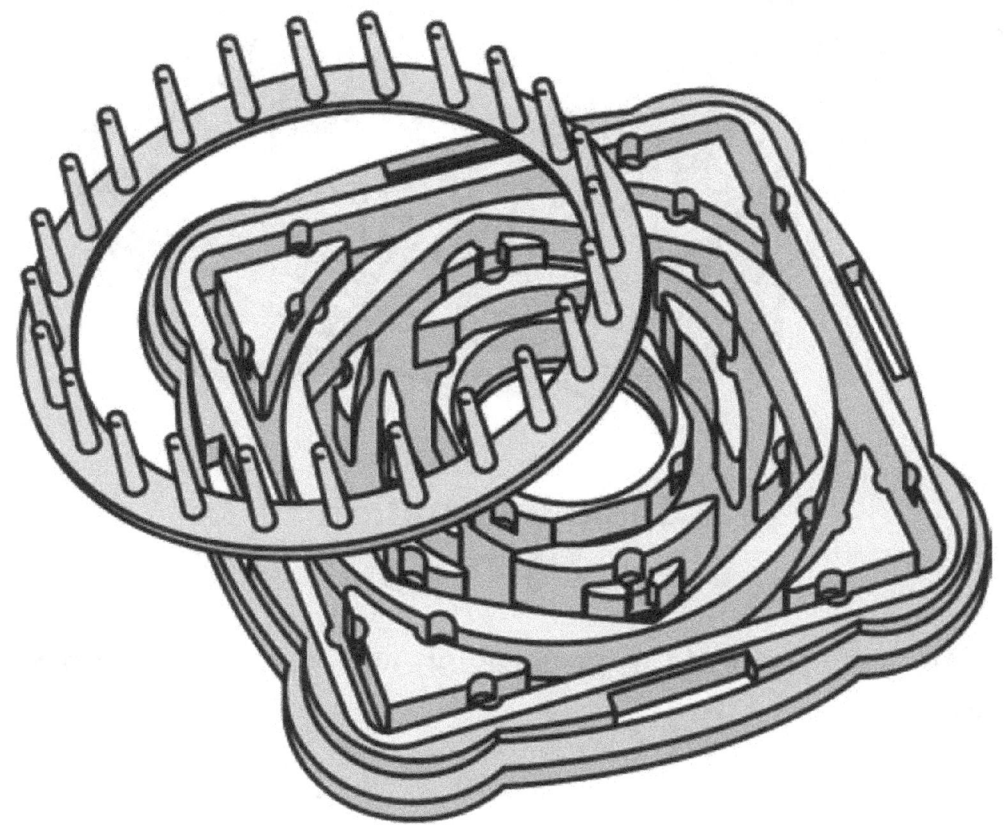

Basic Instruction
Figure 1

2. Thread end of working yarn through the hole on the edge of the base, leaving a 4-inch end. Tie the end and working yarn once over each other to secure the end or make a slip knot in the working yarn to secure yarn at opening on side of base.

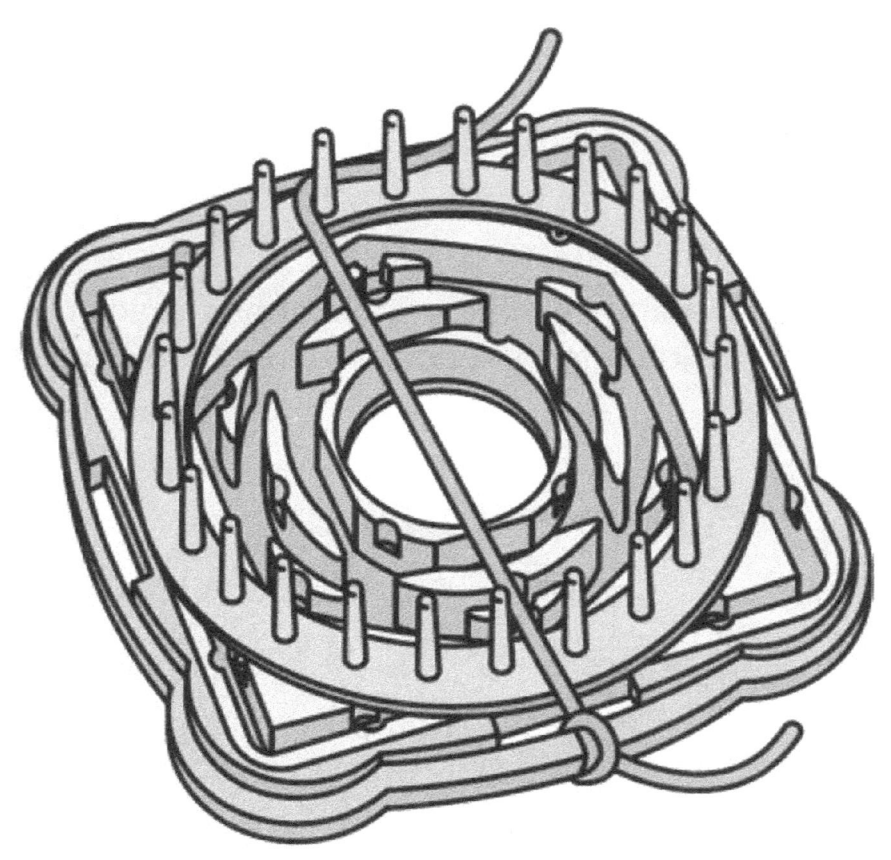

Basic Instruction
Figure 2

3. Wind the yarn around the pegs as shown in How to Wind Yarn instructions.

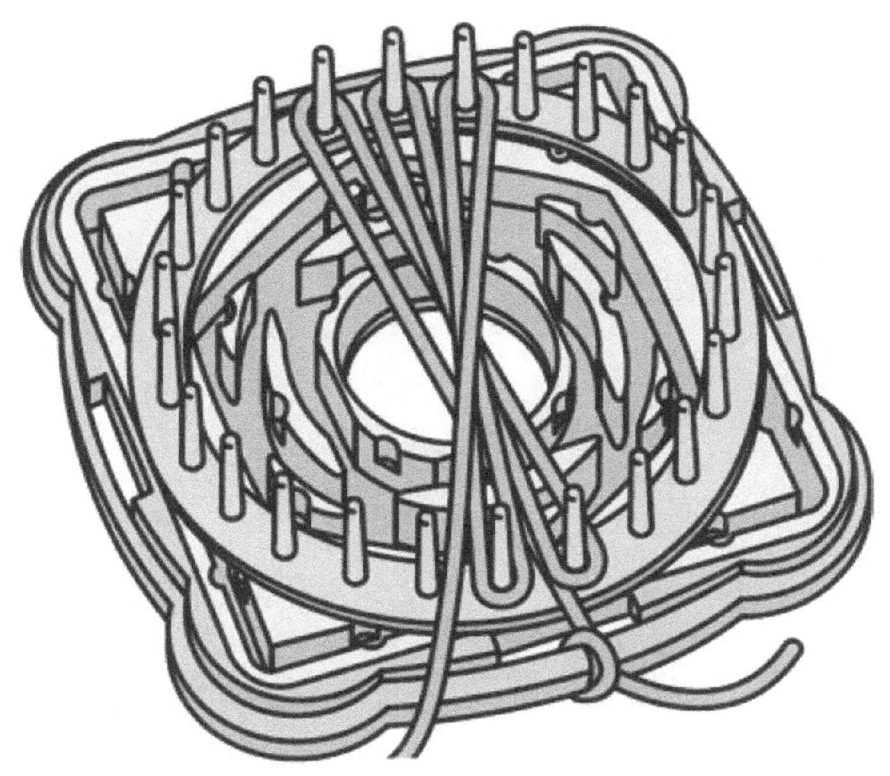

Basic Instruction
Figure 3

4. After winding yarn around all pegs in your pattern, cut yarn, leaving a 4-inch end if using a different yarn for darning. If using the working yarn for darning, leave a 28-inch end. Tie end to the beginning end.

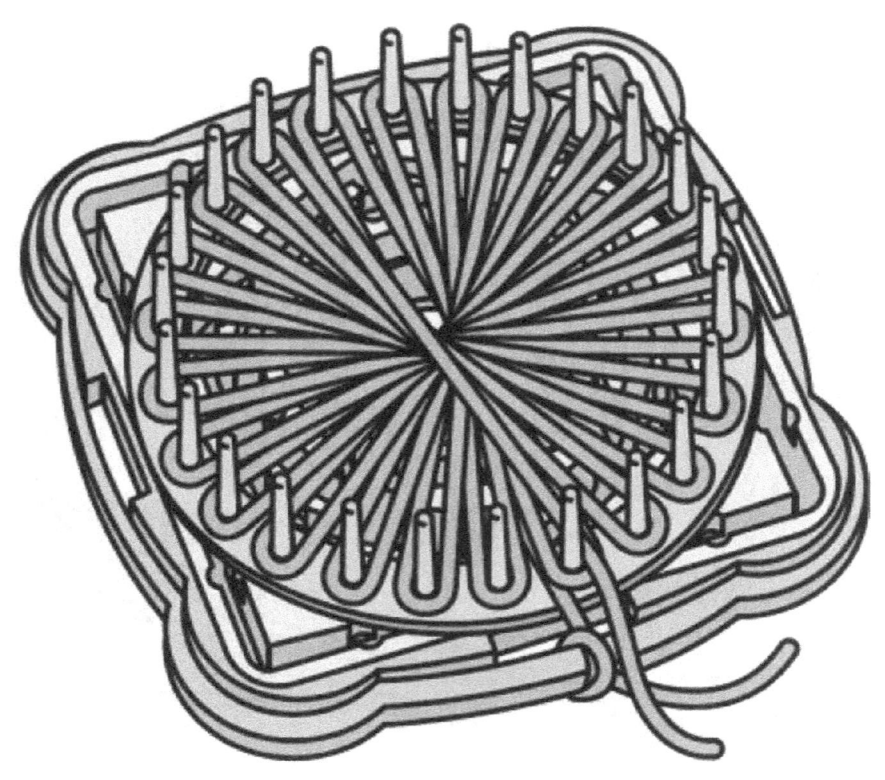

Basic Instruction
Figure 4

5. Thread tapestry needle with a separate strand of yarn and darn as shown in How to Darn: Basic Darning instructions.

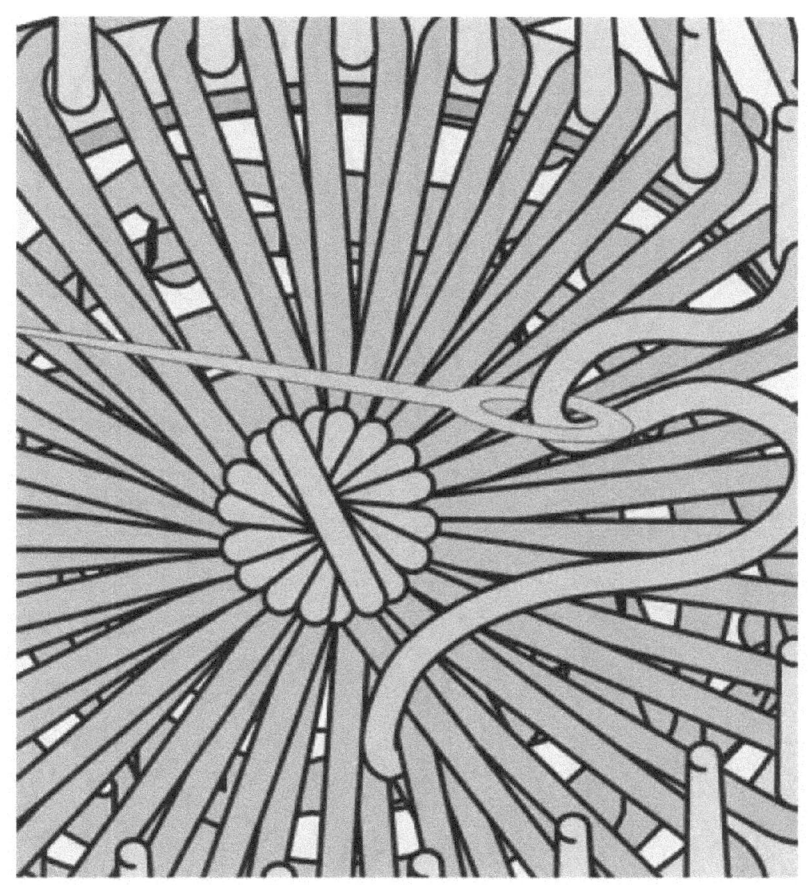

Basic Instruction
Figure 5

6. Remove loom from base; trim and hide ends of yarn. Secure knots with fabric adhesive if desired. Carefully remove flower from loom.

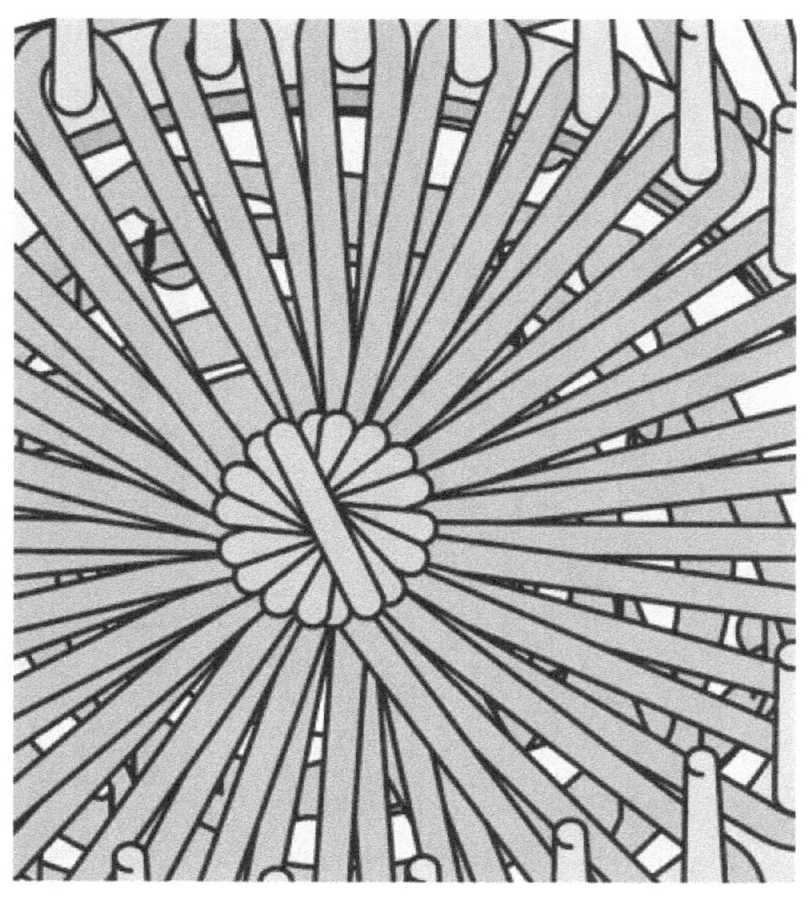

Basic Instruction
Figure 6

How to Wind Yarn

When winding yarn, always wind yarn from left to right (clockwise) around pegs. Hold the yarn down on the last peg wrapped with free hand when moving to next peg. Keep gentle tension on working yarn to keep shape of flower.

1. Bring working yarn straight across the loom from the starting end, making sure the yarn is to the left of the peg closest to the end. Wind yarn around Peg 1 from left to right (clockwise), bringing yarn straight down to Peg 2 on opposite side.

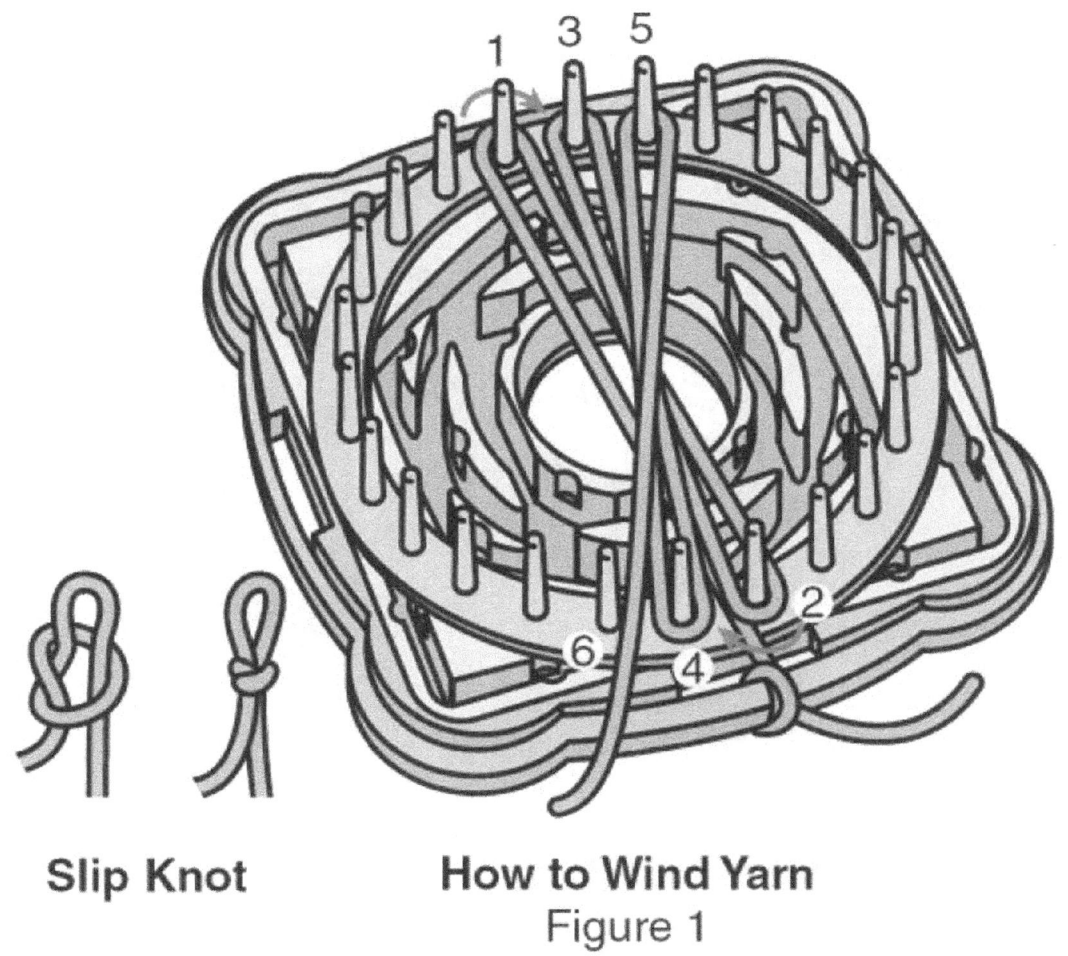

Slip Knot

How to Wind Yarn
Figure 1

2. Continue to wind yarn around pegs in order, alternating sides of loom. Continue in a clockwise fashion until all pegs specified in pattern are wrapped.

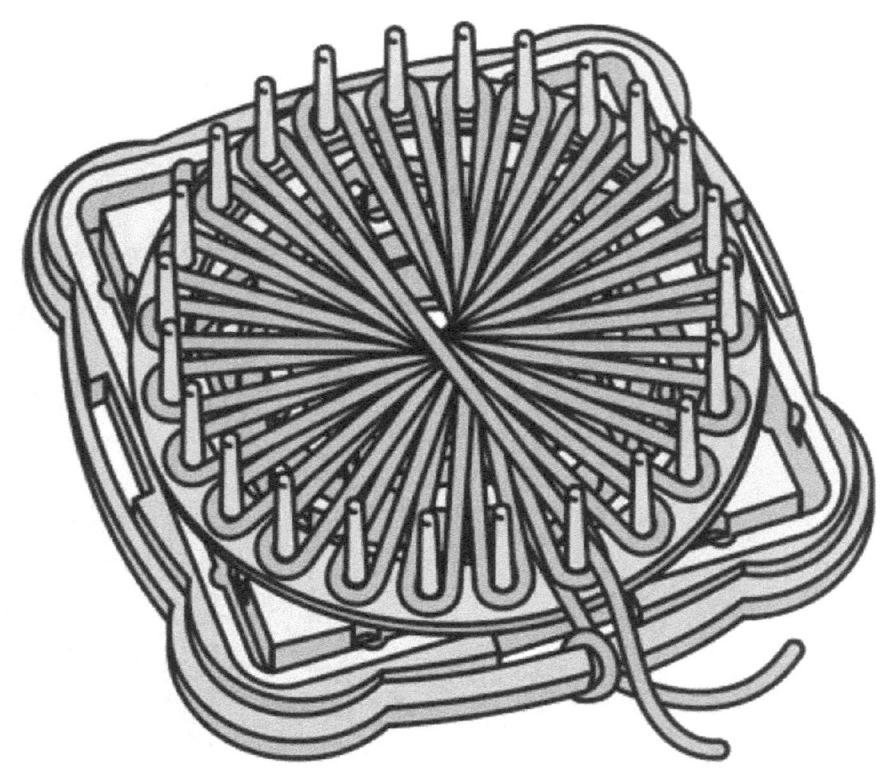

How to Wind Yarn
Figure 2

How to Darn

Basic Darning

1. Thread tapestry needle with strand of darning yarn. Bring the needle up from the back of the base and through the middle of opposite petal last made, leaving a 4-inch end. If using the yarn from the last petal for darning, first bring the long end to the back through the middle of a petal, then follow directions above.

How to Darn
Figure 1

2. Next, insert the needle through the middle of the opposite petal on the front side and pull entire strand through keeping strand tight to create the flower center. This completes one darning stitch.

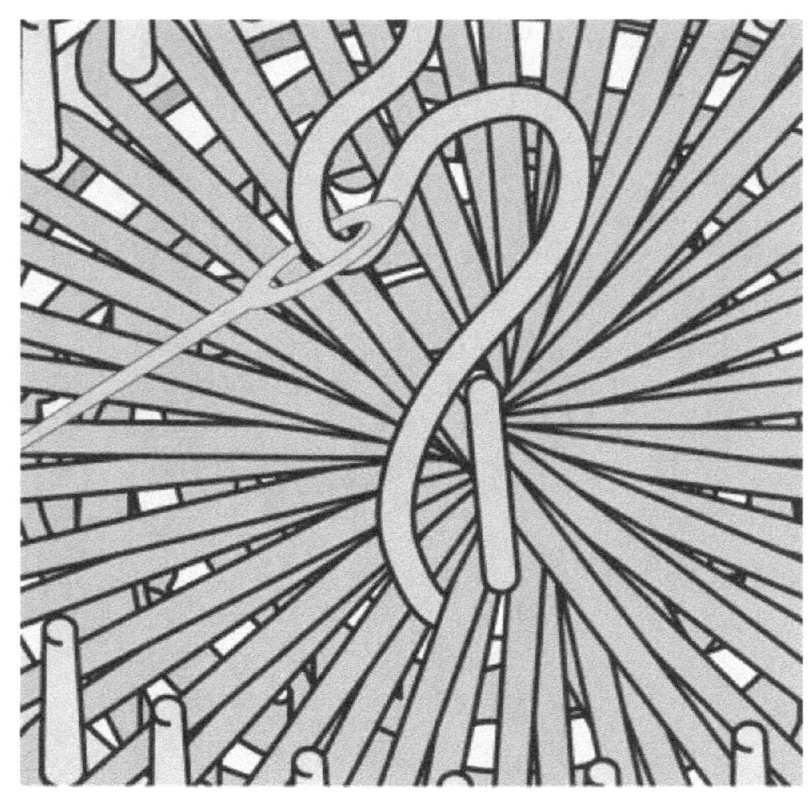

How to Darn
Figure 2

3. Continue to darn each petal around the flower. After all petals are darned, untie yarn ends from loom base.

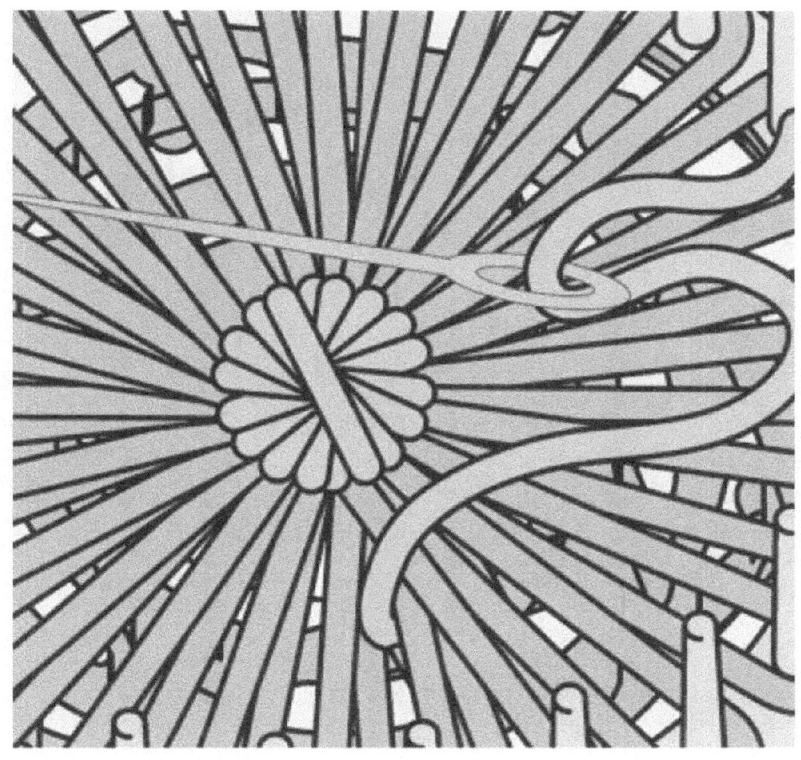

How to Darn
Figure 3

4. To fasten off yarn, pull ends of the yarn to the back side of the loom; tie together and trim. Secure with fabric adhesive if desired.

Backstitch

1. Thread tapestry needle with a strand of yarn 36 inches long.

2. From the top of the loom, insert needle under 4 strands of flower and pull yarn through, leaving a 4-inch beginning tail.

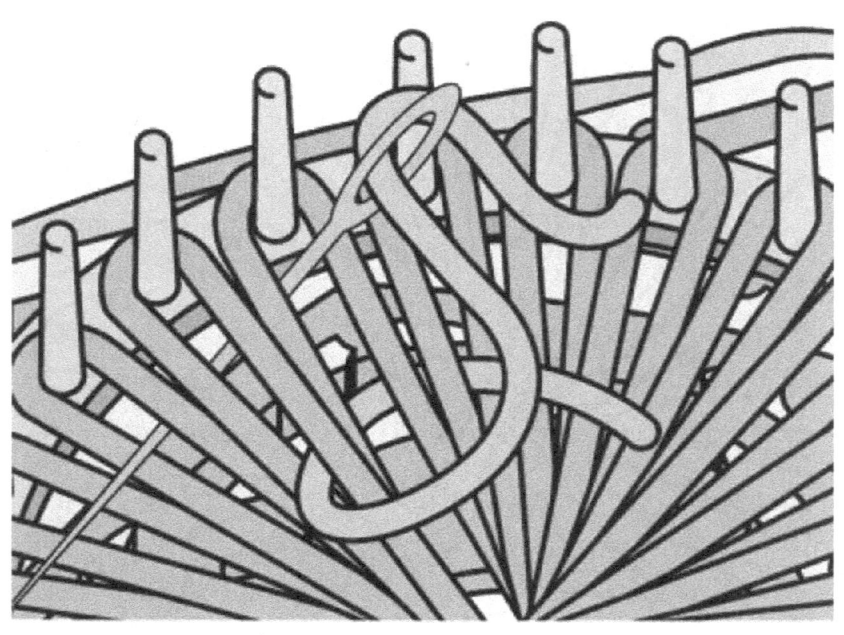

Backstitch
Figure 1

3. Beginning in center of last stitch, insert needle under next 4 strands of Flower and pull yarn through to complete next stitch. Stitch a full circle around flower, keeping each stitch tight and pushed toward center.

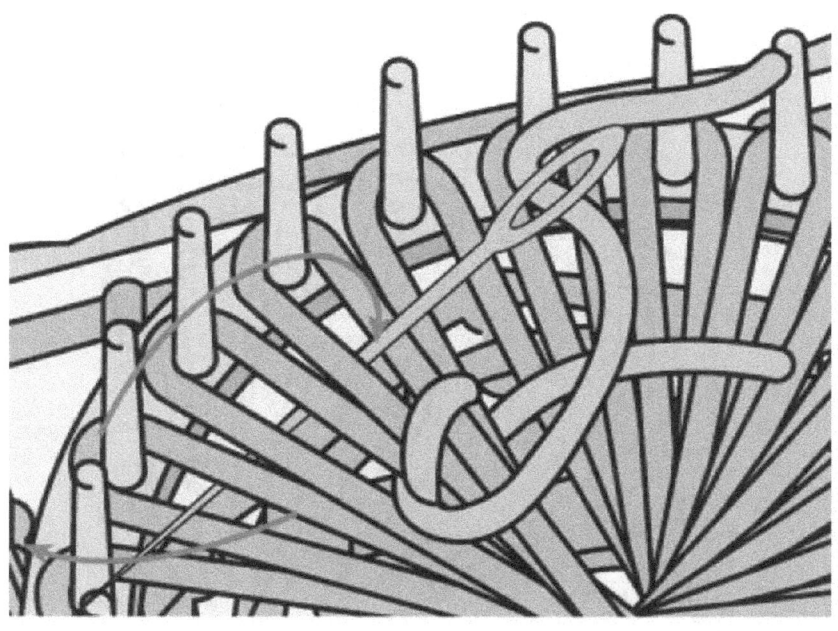

Backstitch
Figure 2

4. To fasten off, tie ends together on back of loom. Weave ends in darning stitches and trim. Secure with fabric adhesive if desired.

Weaving
Darn flower center as shown in How to Darn: Basic Darning to secure flower. Yarn amount varies depending on how much of flower is woven.

1. Thread tapestry needle with strand of desired yarn. Beginning in center of flower, weave working yarn over and under the strands of loops on two pegs. Pull all slack from yarn tight with each stitch.

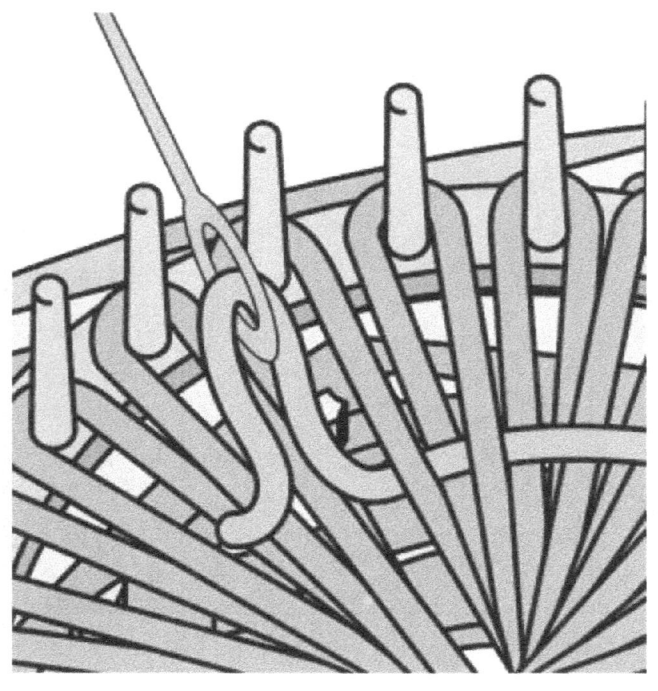

Weaving
Figure 1

2. Weave working yarn under and over the same strands. Always push the weave back firmly toward the center before starting the next row.

Weaving
Figure 2

3. Continue weaving until reaching the desired amount of coverage; fasten ends at back.

4. To fasten off yarn, pull ends of the yarn to the back side of the loom; tie together and trim. Secure with fabric adhesive if desired.

Chain Stitch

1. Darn flower center as shown in How to Darn: Basic Darning to secure flower.

2. Thread tapestry needle with strand of desired yarn 1¼ yards long.

3. From the top of the loom and leaving a 4-inch beginning tail, insert needle under 2 strands of flower—one strand from each petal—and tie together. Push beginning tail to back of loom to the right of knot just made.

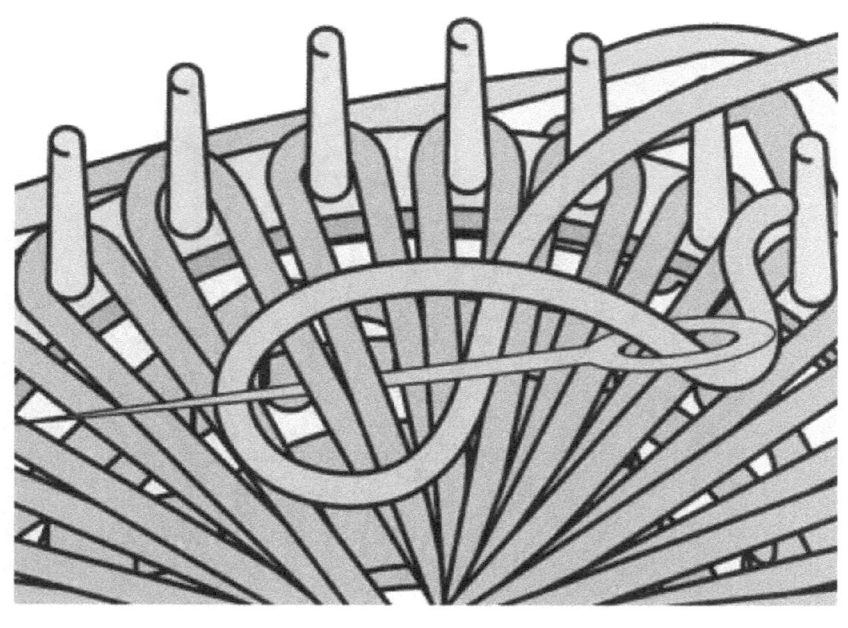

Chain Stitch
Figure 1

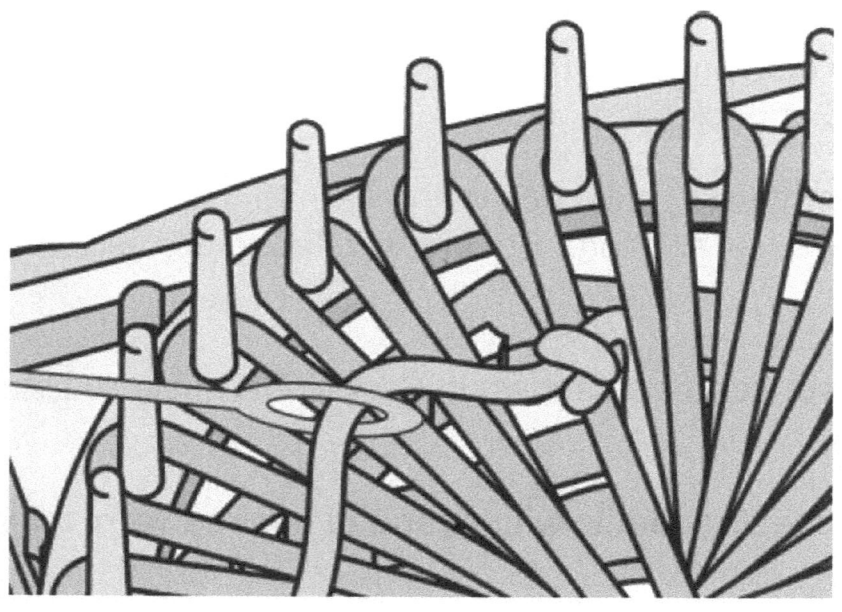

Chain Stitch
Figure 2

4. Make a loose loop of working yarn to lie over the next two neighboring petal loops of flower and toward the left. Insert needle under working loop and next 2 strands of flower. Pull yarn through strands and loop. Tighten loose yarn to create your first chain. Adjust chain as needed to position on flower by sliding stitch with needle.

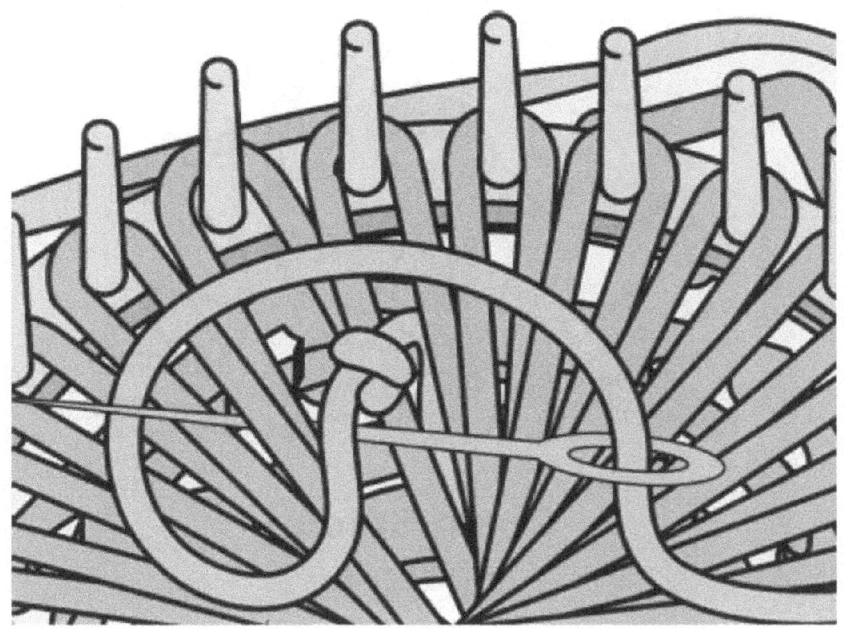

Chain Stitch
Figure 3

5. Continue making loose chain loops and joining next 2 strands of flower as before to create remaining decorative chains on the flower top.

6. On the last set of strands, tie both ends of the darning yarn together in a final knot.

Chain Stitch
Figure 4

7. To fasten off yarn, pull ends of the yarn to the back side of the loom; tie together and trim. Secure with fabric adhesive if desired. ●

Flower Patterns

Use the Flower Patterns along with crochet patterns to complete your projects. All flowers were made using the Hana-Ami Flower Loom from Clover.

Double Layer Flower

There are 24 loops on the main outer layer and 12 loops on the inner layer for a total of 36 loops on this flower. The one-color variation uses 4 yards of yarn. The three-color variation uses 2¼ yards for the outer flower, 1 yard for the inner flower, and 18 inches for darning.

One-Color Variation

1. Follow Basic Instructions section of Flower Loom Instructions article, using large and small loom along with base. Place both looms on base.

2. Wind a flower on the outer loom first following How to Wind Yarn section of Flower Loom Instructions article.

3. Wind a flower on the inner loom.

4. Darn small flower to large flower following How to Darn section of Flower Loom Instructions article.

5. Bring all ends to the back of the loom and tie together. Secure knots with fabric adhesive if desired.

Three-Color Variation

1. Follow Basic Instructions using large and small loom along with base. Place both looms on the base.

2. Wind flower on the outer loom following How To Wind Yarn instructions with first color. Cut first color and secure short tail to the base.

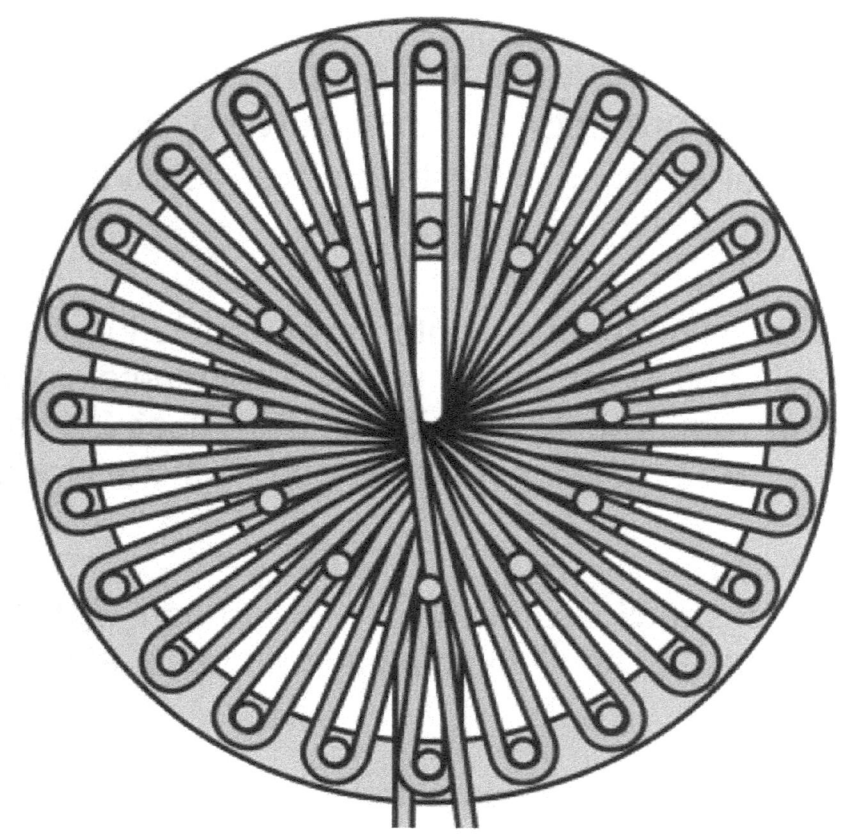

Double Layer Flower
Diagram 1

3. Tie second color to the base opposite from first color. Wind smaller flower with second color. Cut second color and secure short tail to base.

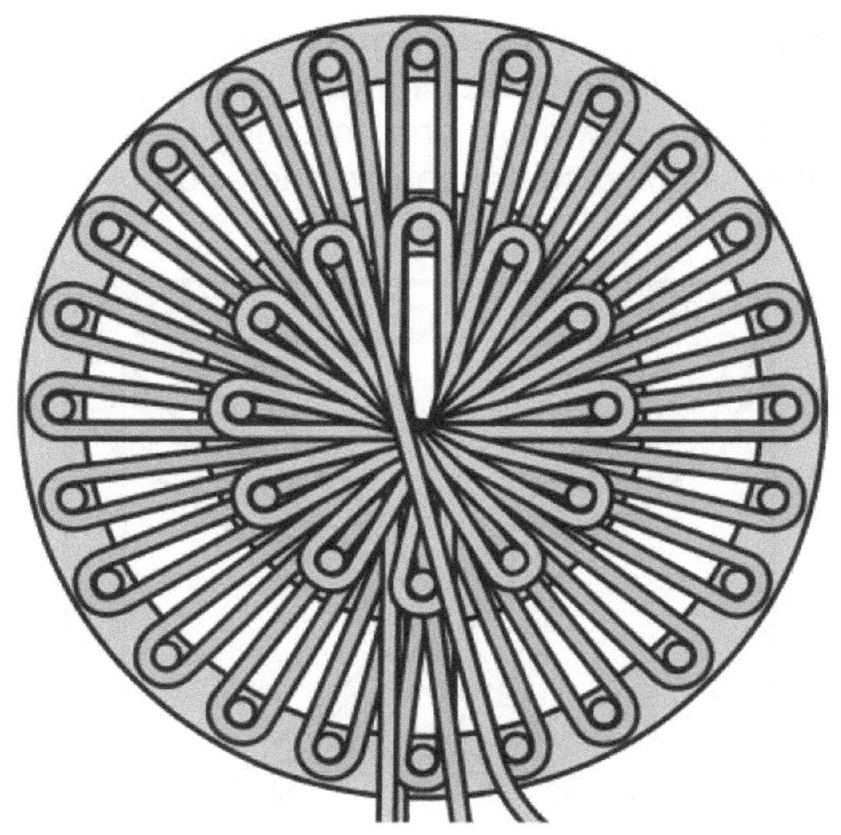

Double Layer Flower
Diagram 2

4. With third color, darn small flower to large flower following How to Darn instructions.

5. Bring all tails to back of loom and tie together. Secure with fabric adhesive if desired.

Diamond Flower

There are 4 long loops (1 at each corner) and 8 side loops for a total of 12 loops on this flower. The flower uses 1½ yards of a single color of yarn.

1. Follow Basic Instructions using smallest square loom along with base. Place loom on base.

2. Tie yarn to base and bring yarn across loom, skipping peg in center of opposite side and wrapping yarn clockwise around peg before corner. Continue winding yarn following How To Wind Yarn instructions and skipping center peg on each side of loom.

Diamond Flower Diagram

3. When completing last petal, bring yarn down and under yarn from peg 6 then wrapping around middle of Flower. Darn center of flower following How to Darn instructions.

4. Bring all tails to back of loom and tie together. Secure with fabric adhesive if desired.

Square & Circle Flower
There are a total of 32 loops on this flower. The two-color variation uses 4 yards for the flower and 3 yards for the darning and decorative stitching.

1. Follow Basic Instructions using largest square loom along with base. Place loom on base.

2. Wind flower on the loom following How to Wind Yarn instructions with first color. Cut first color and secure short tail to the base.

Square & Circle Flower Diagram

3. Darn center of flower following How to Darn instructions and 1 yard of second color. Bring all tails to back of loom and tie together.

4. With 2-yard strand of second color and following Chain Stitch section of Flower Loom Instructions article stitch a full circle around the flower.

Flat Swirl Flower

There are a total of 24 loops on this flower. The two-color variation uses 3 yards for the flower and 2½ yards for darning and decorative stitching.

1. Follow Basic Instructions using largest round loom along with base. Place loom on base.

2. Wind flower on the loom following How to Wind instructions with first color. Cut first color and secure short tail to the base.

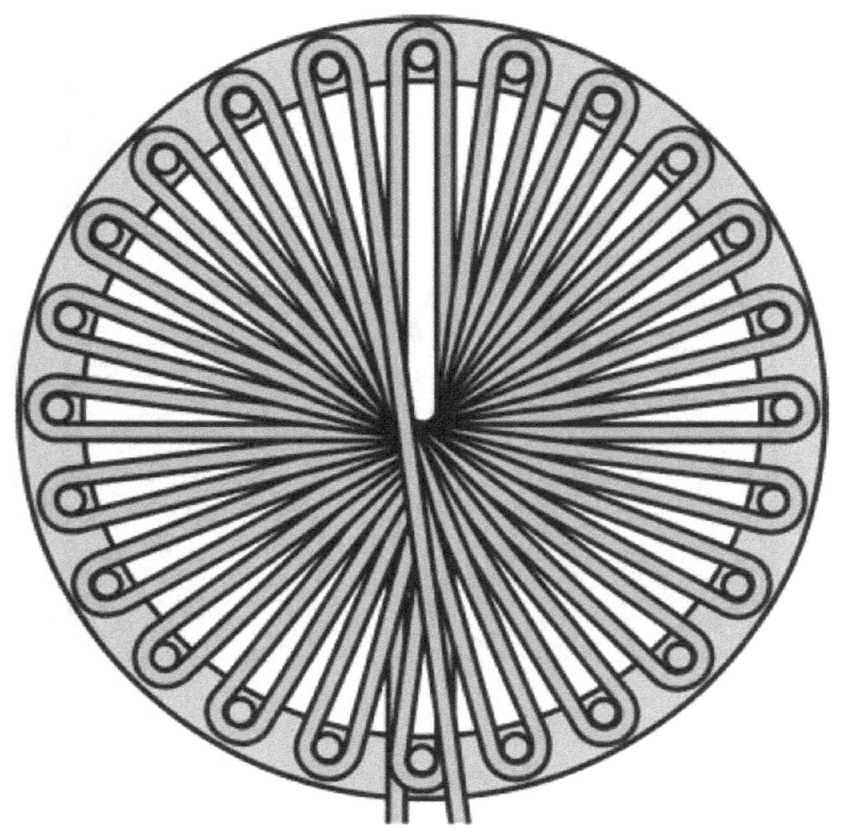

Flat Swirl Flower Diagram

3. With second color, darn center of flower following Backstitch section of Flower Loom Instructions article. Do not cut yarn. Bring all remaining tails to back of loom and tie together.

4. Continuing with second color and following Chain Stitch instructions, stitch a swirl around the flower beginning at center and working chain stitches in a spiral fashion around loom for 6 petals beyond start of swirl or until reaching the edge of the loom.

5. Fasten off yarn in last chain stitch and weave end into body of crochet piece.

Woven Flower

There are a total of 18 loops on this flower. The two-color variation uses 2 yards for the flower and 2 yards for darning and weaving. The three-color variation uses 2 yards for the flower, 1 yard for the darning and 1 yard for the weaving.

Two-Color Variation

1. Follow Basic Instructions using large hexagon loom along with base. Place loom on base.

2. Wind flower on the loom following How to Wind Yarn instructions with first color. Cut first color. Bring tails to back of loom and tie together.

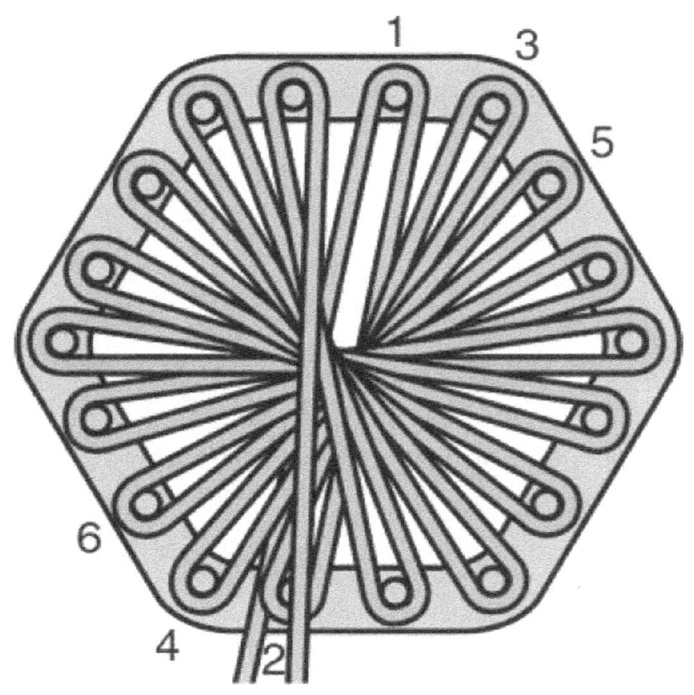

Woven Flower Diagram

3. With second color, darn center of flower following Backstitch instructions. Do not cut yarn. Bring all tails to back of loom and tie together.

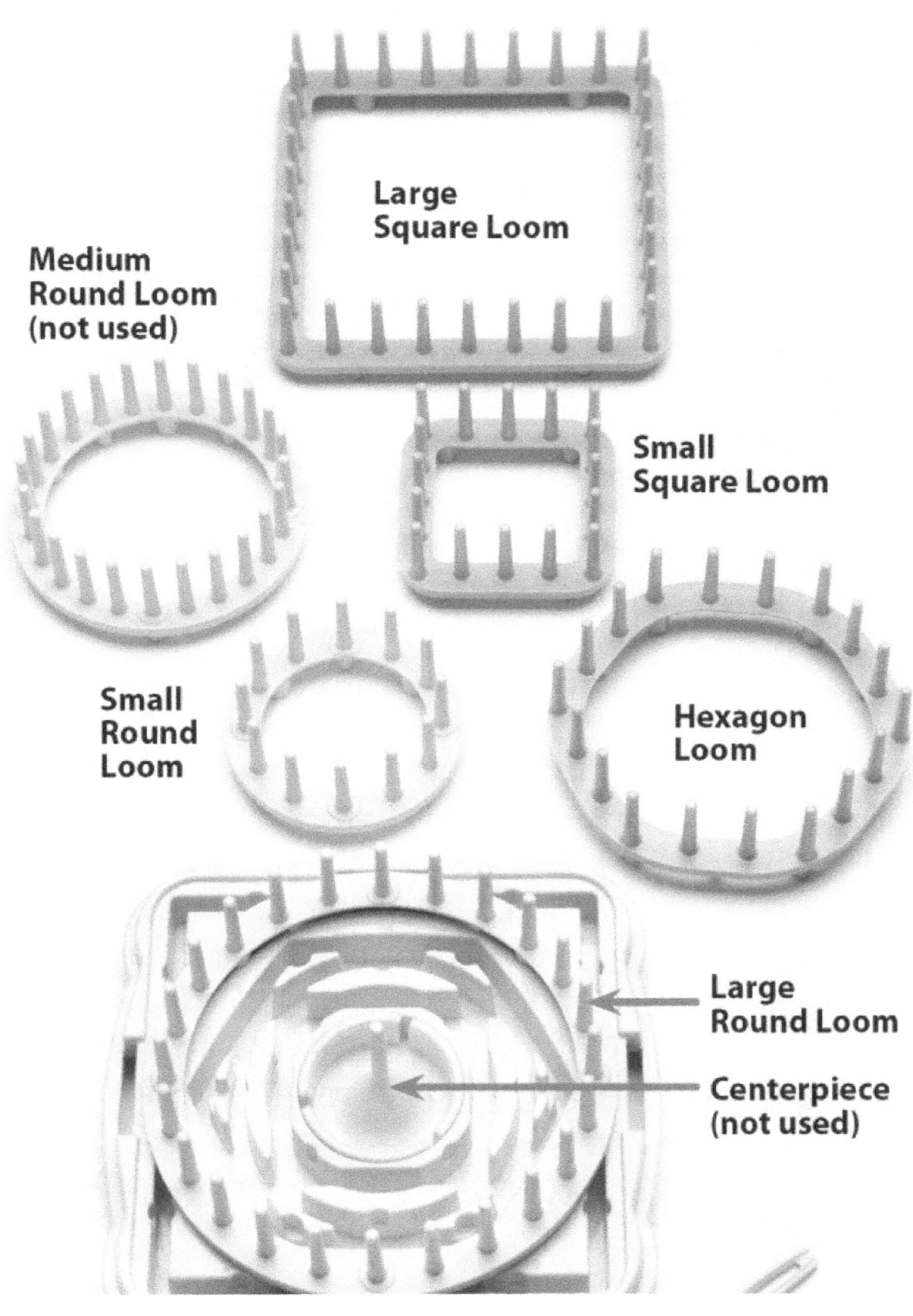

Medium
Round Loom
(not used)

Large
Square Loom

Small
Square Loom

Small
Round
Loom

Hexagon
Loom

Large
Round Loom

Centerpiece
(not used)

4. Continuing with second color and following Weaving section of Flower Loom Instructions article, weave petals beginning with 2 center petals on any side and weaving half of petal or 4 rows.

5. Skip corner petal and weave next 2 petals. Continue weaving until 6 sets of petals are completed.

6. Bring all ends to back of loom and tie together. Secure with fabric adhesive if desired.

Three-Color Variation

1. Follow Basic Instructions using large hexagon loom along with base. Place loom on base.

2. Wind flower on the loom following How to Wind Yarn instructions with first color. Cut first color. Bring tails to back of loom and tie together.

3. With second color, darn center of flower following Backstitch instructions. Cut second color. Bring tails to back of loom and tie together.

4. With third color and following Weaving instructions, weave petals beginning with 2 center petals on any side and weaving half of petal or 4 rows.

5. Skip corner petal and weave next 2 petals. Continue weaving until 6 sets of petals are completed.

6. Bring all ends to back of loom and tie together. Secure with fabric adhesive if desired.

Cute Clutch

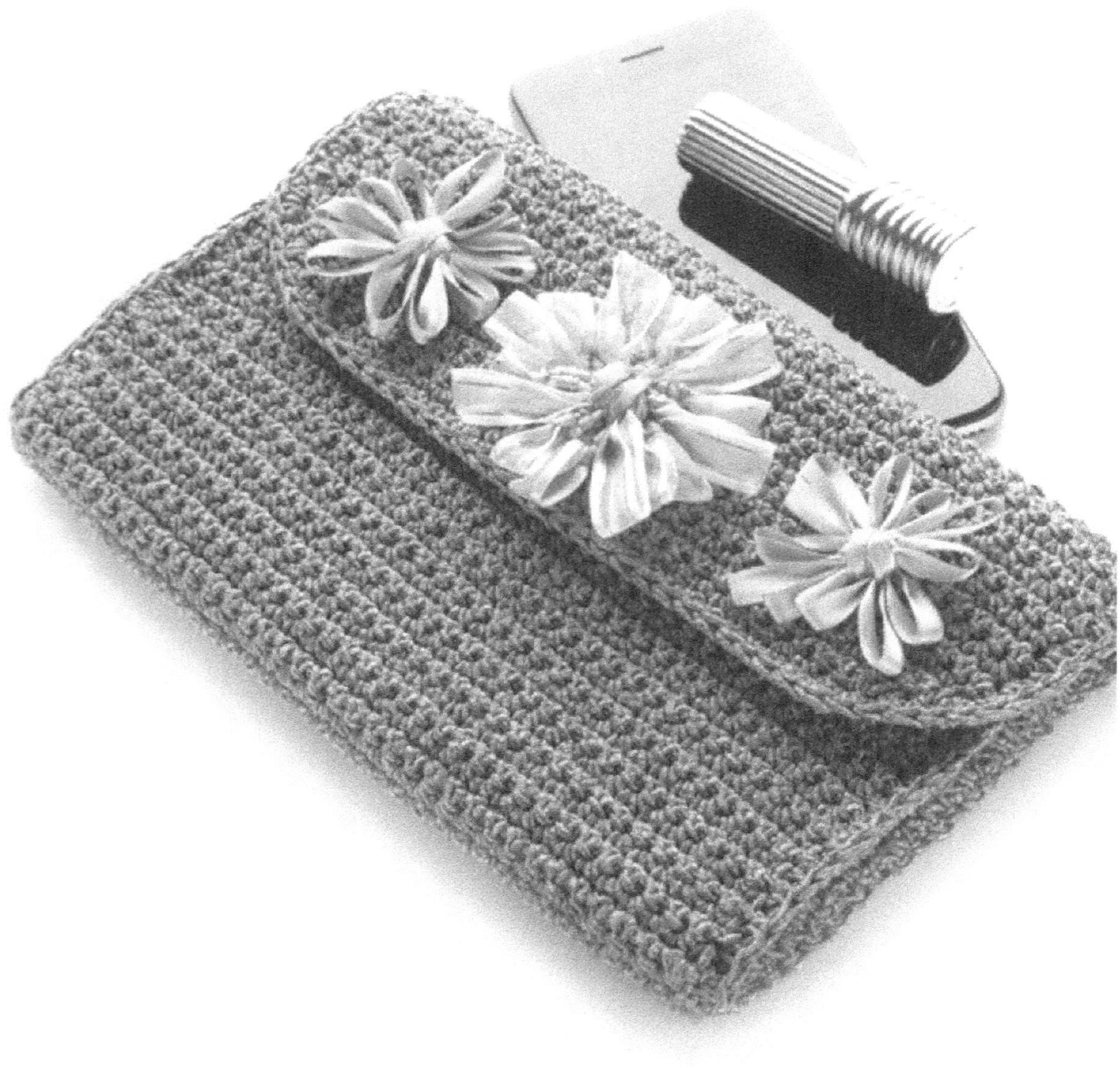

Finished Measurements
8 inches wide x 5 inches tall, with Flap folded

Materials

MEDIUM

- Berroco Captiva medium (worsted) weight cotton/polyester/acrylic yarn (1¾ oz/98 yds/50g per hank): 2 hanks #5558 orchid
- Size H/8/5mm crochet hook or size needed to obtain gauge
- ½-inch gold decorative ribbon: 2 yds
- ¼-inch gold double satin face ribbon: 2 yds
- Tapestry needle
- Hexagon loom
- Smallest round loom
- Small square loom
- Loom base
- Locking stitch marker: 12
- Coordinating fabric for lining: ⅓ yd *(optional)*
- Sewing needle and matching thread *(optional)*
- Snap closure *(optional)*
- Fabric adhesive *(optional)*
- Felt *(optional)*

Gauge

10 sc = 2 inches; 12 rows = 2 inches

Woven Flower = 3 inches in diameter

Diamond Flower = 2 inches corner-to-corner

Pattern Notes

Clutch is made in 3 pieces: 1 Body and 2 Gussets. If desired, a fabric lining and closure can be added.

Place markers as indicated in instructions to mark placement of Gussets.

Join with slip stitch as indicated unless otherwise stated

Clutch

Body

Row 1 (RS): With orchid, ch 37, working in **back bar of ch** *(see illustration)*, sc in 2nd ch from hook and in each rem ch across, turn. **Place marker** *(see Pattern Notes)* in first and last st on row. *(36 sc)*

Back Bar of Chain

Note: Place markers in first and last st of row 28 and row 56.

Rows 2–72: Ch 1, sc in each st across, turn.

Flap

Rows 73–77: Ch 1, **sc dec** *(see Stitch Guide)* in first 2 sts, sc in each rem st across to last 2 sts, sc dec in last 2 sts, turn. *(26 sts at end of row 77)*

At end of last row, fasten off.

Gusset
Make 2.

Row 1: With orchid, ch 17, sc in 2nd ch from hook and in each rem ch across, turn. Place marker in first sc of row 1. *(16 sc)*

Row 2: Ch 1, 2 sc in first sc, sc in each rem sc across, turn. *(17 sc)*

Row 3: Ch 1, sc in each sc across to last sc, 2 sc in last sc, turn. *(18 sc)*

Row 4: Rep row 2. *(19 sc)*

Row 5: Rep row 3. *(20 sc)*

Row 6: Ch 2, place marker in ch-2 just made, sc in each sc across, turn.

Row 7: Ch 1, sc in each sc across to last 2 sc, sc dec in last 2 sc, turn. *(19 sc)*

Row 8: Ch 1, sc dec in first 2 sts, sc in each rem st across, turn. *(18 sts)*

Row 9: Rep row 7. *(17 sts)*

Row 10: Rep row 8, place marker in last st of row. *(16 sts)*

Fasten off.

Flowers
Make 1 Woven Flower referring to Flower Patterns article using a ½-inch ribbon for petals and ¼-inch ribbon for darning.

Make 2 Diamond Flowers referring to Flower Patterns article using ¼-inch ribbon.

Finishing
Weave in ends. Block Clutch pieces to measurements.

Assembly

Using Assembly Diagram as a guide, align Gusset to side of Body with WS tog and pin in place. **Join** *(see Pattern Notes)* orchid at top corner and working through both thicknesses, sc evenly along side, across bottom edge and along opposite side to seam. Fasten off. Rep for 2nd Gusset.

Using photo as a guide, sew Flowers to Clutch.

Lining

Cut piece of fabric 8½ inches wide x 10½ inches long for Body, leaving a ¼-inch seam allowance. Fold fabric in half. Cut 2 pieces of fabric for Gussets, each 2 inches wide x 4¾ inches long with a ¼-inch seam allowance. Using Assembly Diagram as a guide, sew Gussets to Body. Hem top edge of Lining. Place Lining inside Clutch with RS facing and sew in place along hem edge with sewing needle and matching thread.

Closure

Cut 2 circles of felt ¼-inch larger than snap closure. Adhere 1 felt circle to each piece of closure. Position closure to inside of Clutch and working through felt, sew closure in place with sewing needle and matching thread. ●

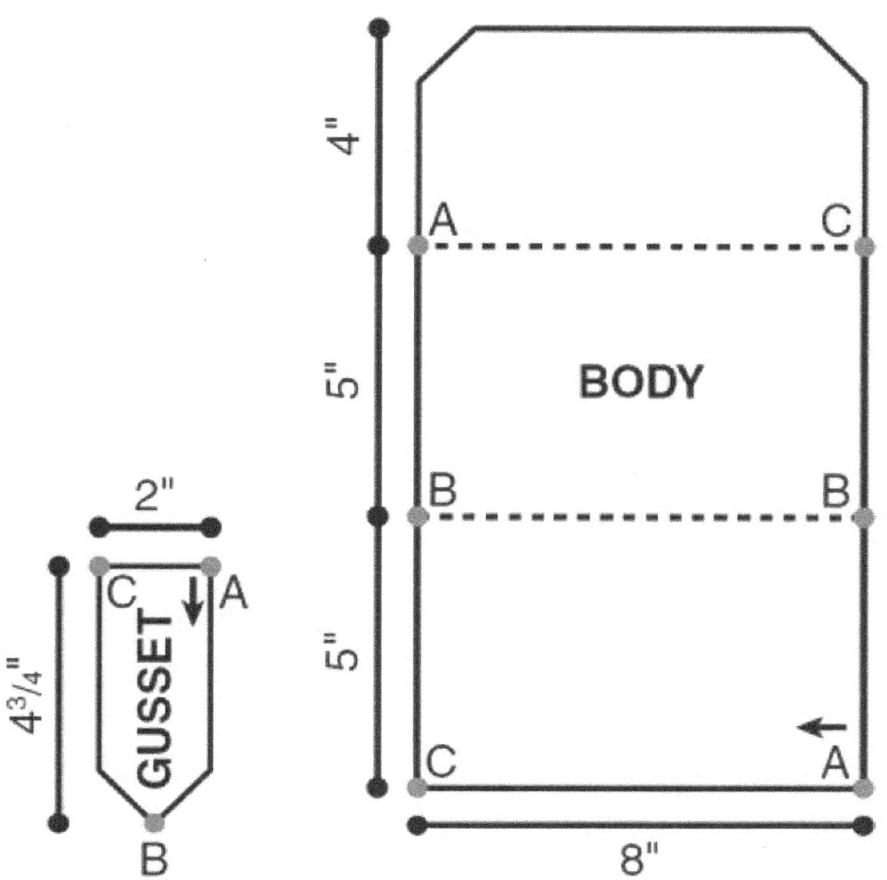

Assembly Diagram
Note: Arrows indicate
direction of work.

Fancy Barrette

Finished Measurement

3 inches in diameter

Materials

MEDIUM

- Wisdom Yarns Poems Silk medium (worsted) weight wool/silk yarn (1¾ oz/109 yds/50g per skein):
    1 skein #737 ribbon reef
- Tapestry needle
- Large round loom
- Small round loom
- Loom base
- ¾-inch decorative button: 1
- Alligator hair clip
- Low temperature hot-glue gun

Gauge

Flower = 3 inches in diameter

Pattern Note

Test hot glue on scrap of project yarn to determine how the yarn will react to heat. If necessary, allow glue to cool on button before adhering to yarn.

Barrette

Flower

Make 1 Double Layer Flower referring to Flower Patterns article and using a single yarn color.

Finishing

Weave in ends. Block lightly if desired.

If needed, carefully remove shank from back of button. Apply glue to back of button. **Allow glue to cool slightly** *(see Pattern Note)* before adhering button to center of Flower.

Slide hair clip through darning on back of Flower. Secure with glue if desired. ●

Cozy Ear Warmer

Finished Sizes

Instructions given fit woman's size small; changes for medium and large are in [ ].

Finished Measurements

Circumference: 18 [20, 22] inches, buttoned

Materials

MEDIUM

- Berroco Vintage medium (worsted) weight acrylic/wool/nylon yarn (3½ oz/217 yds/100g per hank):
    1 hank #51103 clary
    1 yd each #5180 dried plum and #5175 fennel
- Size H/8/5mm crochet hook or size needed to obtain gauge
- Tapestry needle
- Sewing needle

- Matching sewing thread
- Hexagon loom and base
- ⅝-inch button: 2

Gauge
8 sc = 2 inches; 9 rows = 2 inches

Pattern Notes
Chain-1 at beginning of row does not count as a stitch unless otherwise stated.

Chain-2 at beginning of row does not count as a stitch unless otherwise stated.

Chain-3 at beginning of row counts as first double crochet unless otherwise stated.

Join with slip stitch as indicated unless otherwise stated.

Special Stitch
Split double crochet decrease (split dc dec): Yo, insert hook in next st, yo and pull up lp, yo, draw through 2 lps on hook, sk next st, yo, insert hook in next st, yo and pull up lp, yo, draw through 2 lps on hook, yo, draw through all 3 lps on hook.

Ear Warmer
Row 1: With clary, ch 4, sc in 2nd ch from hook and in each of next 2 chs, turn. *(3 sc)*

Row 2: Ch 1 *(see Pattern Notes)*, sc in each sc across, turn.

Row 3: Ch 1, sc in next sc, 2 sc in next sc, sc in next sc, turn. *(4 sc)*

Row 4: Rep row 2.

Row 5: Ch 1, sc in next sc, 2 sc in next sc, sc in each of next 2 sc, turn. *(5 sc)*

Rows 6–10: [Rep row 2] 5 times.

Row 11: Ch 1, sc in next sc, 2 sc in next sc, sc in next sc, 2 sc in next sc, sc in next sc, turn. *(7 sc)*

Rows 12–15: [Rep row 2] 4 times.

Row 16: Ch 1, sc in next sc, 2 sc in next sc, sc in each of next 3 sc, 2 sc in next sc, sc in next sc, turn. *(9 sc)*

Rows 17–20: [Rep row 2] 4 times.

Row 21: Ch 1, hdc in each of next 4 sc, (hdc, ch 1, hdc) in next sc, hdc in each of next 4 sc, turn. *(10 hdc, 1 ch-1 sp)*

Row 22: Ch 1, hdc in each of next 5 hdc, (hdc, ch 1, hdc) in next ch-1 sp, hdc in each of next 5 hdc, turn. *(12 hdc, 1 ch-1 sp)*

Row 23: Ch 2 *(see Pattern Notes)*, sk first hdc, dc in each of next 5 hdc, (dc, ch 1, dc) in next ch-1 sp, dc in each of next 4 hdc, **dc dec** *(see Stitch Guide)* in next 2 hdc, turn. *(12 sts, 1 ch-1 sp)*

Rows 24 & 25: Ch 2, sk first st, dc in each of next 5 sts, (dc, ch 1, dc) in next ch-1 sp, dc in each of next 4 sts, dc dec in last 2 sts, turn.

Row 26: Ch 2, sk first st, dc in each of next 5 sts, (dc, ch 2, dc) in next ch-1 sp, dc in each of next 4 sts, dc dec in last 2 sts, turn. *(12 sts, 1 ch-2 sp)*

Row 27: Ch 2, sk first st, dc in each of next 5 sts, (2 dc, ch 1, 2 dc) in next ch-2 sp, dc in each of next 4 sts, dc dec in last 2 sts, turn. *(14 sts, 1 ch-1 sp)*

Rows 28–33 [28–34, 28–35]: Ch 2, sk first st, dc in each of next 6 sts, (dc, ch 1, dc) in next ch-1 sp, dc in each of next 5 sts, dc dec in last 2 sts, turn.

Center Top

Row 34 [35, 36]: Ch 2, sk first st, dc in each of next 6 sts, 2 dc in next ch-1 sp, dc in each of next 5 sts, dc dec in last 2 sts, turn. *(14 sts)*

Row 35 [36, 37]: Ch 2, dc in each st across, turn.

Row 36 [37, 38]: Ch 2, dc in each of next 6 sts, dc dec in next 2 sts, dc in each of next 6 sts, turn. *(13 sts)*

Rows 37–42 [38–44, 39–46]: Ch 3 *(see Pattern Notes)*, dc in first st, dc in each of next 4 sts, **split dc dec** *(see Special Stitch)* in next 3 sts, dc in each of next 4 sts, 2 dc in last st, turn.

Row 43 [45, 47]: Ch 3, dc in first st, dc in each of next 3 sts, dc dec in next 2 sts, sk next st, dc dec in next 2 sts, dc in each of next 3 sts, 2 dc in last st, turn. *(12 sts)*

Rows 44–47 [46–49, 48–51]: Ch 3, dc in first st, dc in each of next 3 sts, [dc dec in next 2 sts] twice, dc in each of next 3 sts, 2 dc in last st, turn.

Row 48 [50, 52]: Ch 1, hdc in each of next 5 sts, dc dec in next 2 sts, hdc in each of next 5 sts, turn. *(11 sts)*

Row 49 [51, 53]: Ch 1, hdc in each of next 5 sts, sk next st, hdc in each of next 5 sts, turn. *(10 sts)*

Rows 50–53 [52–55, 54–57]: Ch 1, sc in each st across, turn.

Row 54 [56, 58]: Ch 1, sc in each of next 4 sts, **sc dec** *(see Stitch Guide)* in next 2 sts, sc in each of next 4 sts, turn. *(9 sts)*

Row 55 [57, 59]: Ch 1, sc in each st across, turn.

Row 56 [58, 60]: Ch 1, sc in first st, sc dec in next 2 sts, sc in each of next 3 sts, sc dec in next 2 sts, sc in last st, turn. *(7 sts)*

Rows 57–59 [59–61, 61–64]: Ch 1, sc in each st across, turn.

Row 60 [62, 65]: Ch 1, sc in first sc, sc dec in next 2 sts, sc in next st, sc dec in next 2 sts, sc in the next st, turn. *(5 sts)*

Row 61 [63, 66]: Ch 1, sc in each st across, turn.

Row 62 [64, 67]: Ch 1, sc in first st, sc dec in next 2 sts, sc in each of next 2 sts, turn. *(4 sts)*

Row 63 [65, 68]: Ch 1, sc in each st across, turn.

Row 64 [66, 69]: Ch 1, sc in first st, sc dec in next 2 sts, sc in next st, turn. *(3 sc)*

Row 65 [67, 70]: Ch 1, sc in each st across, turn.

Edging

Rnd 1: Now working in rnds, sc evenly in row ends along side of piece, 2 sc in corner of row 1, ch 4 *(button loop made)*, sk next 2 sc on row 1, 2 sc in next corner, sc evenly in row ends along opposite side, 2 sc in corner of last row, ch 4 *(button loop made)*, sk next 2 sc on last row, sc in last sc, **join** *(see Pattern Notes)* in first sc. Fasten off.

Flower

Make 1 Woven Flower referring to Flower Patterns article and using plum for petals, fennel for darning and clary for weaving.

Finishing

With sewing needle and matching thread, sew 1 button on end of Ear Warmer 1 inch from inside edge. Sew 1 button on opposite end of piece 1 inch from outside edge. Secure with button loops. ●

Rustic Brooch

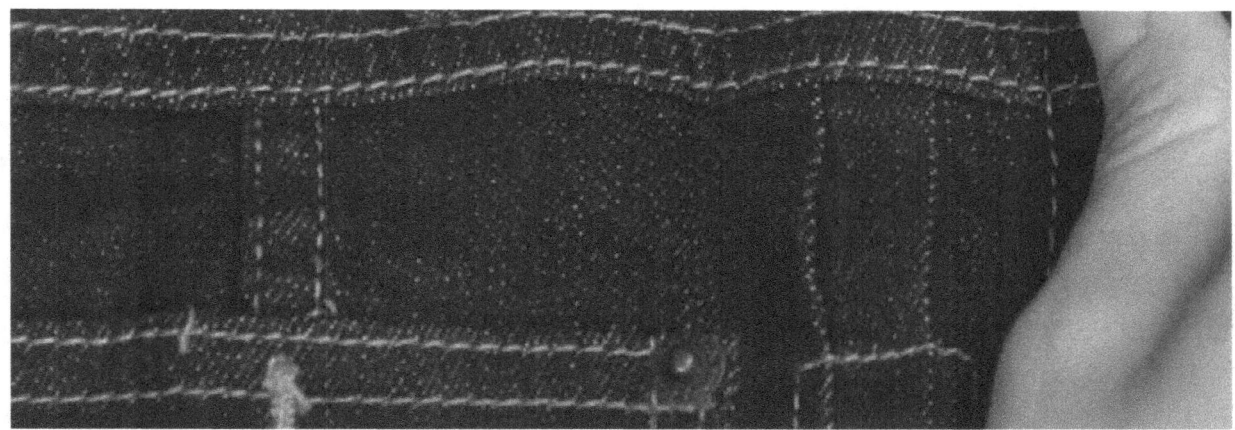

 EASY

Finished Measurement

2¾ inches in diameter

Materials

MEDIUM

- Premier Yarns Home Raffia medium (worsted) weight cellulose rayon yarn (1¼ oz/87 yds/35g per ball):
    1 ball #9905 hollow reeds
- Tapestry needle
- Hexagon loom
- Loom base
- 1-inch nickel-plated flat round pin back
- Low temperature hot-glue gun
- 1-inch round piece matching felt (optional)
- Permanent fabric adhesive (optional)

Gauge

Flower = 2¾ inches in diameter

Pattern Notes

Use felt and fabric adhesive if making Flower with yarn or ribbon.

Brooch shown is made with raffia yarn and does not use felt or adhesive glue.

Brooch

Flower

Make 1 Woven Flower referring to Flower Patterns article and using a **single yarn color** *(see Pattern Notes)*.

Finishing

Weave in ends. Block lightly if using yarn or ribbon.

If needed, trim felt to shape of pin backing. Glue felt to back of flower with fabric adhesive, allowing glue to dry completely.

Glue Flower to pin backing with low temperature hot-glue gun.

Swirl Beret

Skill Level

■■■▢ INTERMEDIATE

Finished Sizes

Instructions given fit woman's small; changes for medium and large are in [ ].

Finished Measurements

Circumference: 18 [21, 24] inches

Materials

MEDIUM

- HiKoo Yarns SimpliCria medium (worsted) weight baby alpaca yarn (⅞ oz/95 yds/25g per ball):
    2 balls #251 purple/blue heather
    1 ball #250 peach/pink heather
- Size I/9/5.5mm crochet hook or size needed to obtain gauge
- Tapestry needle
- Large round loom

- Loom base
- Locking stitch marker

Gauge

16 sc = 4 inches

Flower = 3-inch diameter

Pattern Notes

Join with slip stitch as indicated unless otherwise stated.

Hat is worked in continuous rounds; do not join or turn at end of each round.

Place marker in last stitch of round; move marker as work progresses.

Special Stitch

V-stitch (V-st): (Dc, ch 2, dc) in indicated st or sp.

Beret

Flower

Make 1 Flat Swirl Flower referring to Flower Patterns article using peach for flower and purple for darning and decorative stitching.

Hat

Rnd 1: Join purple in same lp on Flower as last decorative ch st, ch 1, sc in same lp, [ch 2, sc in next Flower lp] 6 times, [ch 2, hdc in next Flower lp] 17 times, ch 2, **do not join** (see Pattern Notes). **Place marker in last ch** (see Pattern Notes). (7 sc, 17 hdc, 24 ch-2 sps)

Rnd 2: (Dc, ch 3) in each ch-2 sp around. (24 dc, 24 ch-3 sps)

Rnd 3: V-st *(see Special Stitch)* in each ch-3 sp around. *(24 V-sts)*

Rnd 4: V-st in ch-2 sp of each V-st around.

Rnd 5: [Ch 1, V-st in ch-2 sp of next V-st] around. *(24 ch-1 sps, 24 V-sts)*

Rnd 6: [Ch 2, 3 dc in ch-2 sp of next V-st] around. *(24 ch-2 sps, 72 dc)*

Rnd 7: [(Dc, ch 3, dc) in next ch-2 sp, dc in each of next 3 dc] around. *(120 dc, 24 ch-3 sps)*

Rnd 8: [3 dc in next ch-3 sp, sk next 2 dc, 3 dc in next dc] around. *(48 3-dc grps)*

Rnd 9: Dc in each dc around. *(144 dc)*

Rnd 10: Hdc in each dc around.

Rnd 11: Sc in each hdc around.

Rnd 12: Sc in each sc around.

Rnd 13: [Sc in each of next 10 sc, **sc dec** *(see Stitch Guide)* in next 2 sc] around. *(132 sts)*

Rnd 14: [Sc in each of next 9 sts, sc dec in next 2 sts] around. *(120 sts)*

Rnd 15: [Sc in each of next 8 sts, sc dec in next 2 sts] around. *(108 sts)*

Rnd 16: [Sc in each of next 7 sts, sc dec in next 2 sts] around. *(96 sts)*

Sizes Small & Medium Only

Rnd 17: [Sc in each of next 6 sts, sc dec in next 2 sts] around. *(84 sts)*

Rnd 18: [Sc in each of next 5 sts, sc dec in next 2 sts] around. *(72 sts)*

All Sizes
Rnd 19 [18, 17]: Sc in each st around. *(72 [84, 96] sc)*

Rnds 20 & 21 [19 & 20, 18 & 19]: Hdc in each st around. *(72 [84, 96] hdc)*

Rnds 22 & 23 [21 & 22, 20 & 21]: Sc in each st around. At end of last rnd, sl st in each of next 3 sts. *(72 [84, 96] dc)*

Fasten off.

Finishing
Weave in ends. Block lightly if desired. ●

Petal Shawl

Skill Level

 **INTERMEDIATE**

Finished Measurements

56 inches wide x 19 inches long

Materials

- Berroco Mixer fine (sport) weight cotton/polyester/rayon/viscose/nylon yarn (1¾ oz/165 yds/50g per hank):
    3 hanks #8144 jive

FINE

- Aunt Lydia's Classic Crochet size 10 crochet cotton (350 yds per ball):
    1 ball #495 wood violet

LACE

- Size C/2/2.75mm crochet hook or size needed to obtain gauge
- Tapestry needle
- Large round loom
- Smallest round loom
- Loom base
- Permanent fabric adhesive

Gauge
14 chs = 2 inches

Pattern Notes
Use fabric adhesive to secure knots on back of Flowers.

Join with slip stitch as indicated unless otherwise stated.

A double petal is made from 2 loops on outer flower of Double Layer Flower. Double Layer Flower has 12 double petals.

A long petal is 1 loop at corner on Diamond Flower. The remaining loops are petals. The Diamond Flower has 4 long petals and 8 petals.

Special Stitches
Double crochet double treble crochet decrease (dc-dtr dec): Holding last lp of each st on hook, dc in indicated sp, **dtr** *(see Stitch Guide)* in next joining sl st, yo and draw through last 3 lps on hook.

Double treble crochet double crochet decrease (dtr-dc dec): Holding last lp of each st on hook, dtr in joining sl st, dc in indicated sp, yo and draw through last 3 lps on hook.

Single crochet join (sc join): Place slip knot on hook, insert hook in indicated st, yo and draw up a lp, yo and draw through both lps on hook.

Shawl

With jive, make 70 Double Layer Flowers and 49 Diamond Flowers referring to Flower Patterns article.

First Row

First Double Layer Flower

Join *(see Pattern Notes)* violet in any **double petal** *(see Pattern Notes)*, [ch 7, sl st in next double petal] 4 times, ch 7, leave rem double petals unworked.

2nd Double Layer Flower

Sl st in any double petal of next Flower, ch 3, sl st in ch-7 sp just made, ch 3, sl st in next double petal on same Flower, [ch 7, sl st in next double petal on same Flower] 5 times, ch 7, leave rem double petals unworked.

3rd–15th Double Layer Flowers

Work as for 2nd Double Layer Flower.

16th Double Layer Flower

Sl st in any double petal on Last Flower, ch 3, sl st in ch-7 sp just made, ch 3, sl st in next double petal on same Flower, [ch 7, sl st in next double petal on same Flower] 10 times, do not fasten off.

Bottom Edging

Now working across bottom of each Flower on First Row Edging, *ch 3, sl st in next ch-7 sp between Flowers, ch 3, sl st in double petal on next Flower, [ch 7, sl st in next double petal on same Flower] 4 times, rep from * across row to First Flower, ch 3, sl st in ch-7 sp between Flowers, ch 3, sl st in next double petal on First Flower, [ch 7, sl st in next double petal on same Flower] 6 times, ch 7, join in first sl st. Fasten off.

2nd Row

First Diamond Flower

Join violet in petal to right of any **long petal** *(see Pattern Notes)* on First Diamond Flower, ch 1, (sl st, ch 7, sl st) in next long petal, ch 1, sl st in next petal, ch 7, sl st in next petal, ch 1, (sl st, ch 3, sl st in 2nd ch-7 sp before join between Double Layer Flowers, ch 3, sl st) in next long petal, ch 1, sl st in next petal, ch 3, sl st in next ch-7 sp, ch 3, sl st in next petal, ch 1, (sl st, ch 3, sl st in joining sl st between next 2 Double Layer Flowers, ch 3, sl st) in next long petal, ch 1, sl st in next petal, ch 3, sl st in next ch-7 sp, ch 3, sl st in next petal, ch 1, (sl st, ch 3, sl st in next ch-7 sp, ch 3, sl st) in next long petal, ch 1, sl st in next petal, ch 7, join in first st. Fasten off.

2nd–15th Diamond Flowers

Work as for First Diamond Flower, working between Double Layer Flowers and using Assembly Diagram as a guide.

3rd Row

First Double Layer Flower

Join violet in any double petal, [ch 7, sl st in next double petal] 3 times, ch 3, sl st in ch-7 sp before joining sl st between adjacent Double Layer Flower and Diamond Flower, ch 3, sl st in next double petal, ch 3, sl st in joining sl st between adjacent Double Layer Flower and Diamond Flower, ch 3, sl st in next double petal, [ch 3, sl st in next ch-7 sp on adjacent Diamond Flower, ch 3, sl st in next double petal] twice, ch 7, do not fasten off.

2nd Double Layer Flower

*Sl st in any double petal, ch 3, sl st in joining sl st on previous Double Layer Flower and adjacent Diamond Flower, ch 3, sl st in next double petal, ch 3, sl st in next ch-7 sp on adjacent Diamond Flower, ch 3, sl st in next double petal, ch 3, sl st in next joining sl st between adjacent Diamond Flower and next Double Layer Flower, ch 3, sl st in next double petal**, ch 3, sl st in next joining sl st between adjacent Double Layer Flower and next Diamond Flower, ch 3, sl st in next double petal, [ch 3, sl st in next ch-7 sp on Diamond Flower, ch 3, sl st in next double petal] twice, ch 7, do not fasten off. 7 double petals are joined on each adjacent Double Layer flower.

3rd–15th Double Layer Flowers

Work as for 2nd Double Layer Flower.

16th Double Layer Flower

Work as for 2nd Double Layer Flower from * to **, ch 3, sl st in next ch-7 sp on adjacent Diamond Flower, ch 3, sl st in next double petal, [ch 7, sl st in next double petal] 7 times, do not fasten off.

Bottom Edging

Now working across bottom of each Flower on 2nd Row, *ch 3, sl st in ch-7 sp between first 2 Double Layer Flowers, ch 3, sl st in next double petal, [ch 7, sl st in next double petal] 4 times, rep from * across, join in first sl st. Fasten off.

4th–11th Rows

Work as for 2nd and 3rd rows referring to Assembly Diagram for Flower type and placement.

Top Border

Row 1: With WS facing, **sc join** *(see Special Stitches)* violet in ch-7 sp at top of first Flower, ch 5, sc in next ch-7 sp, *ch 7, **dc-dtr dec** *(see Special Stitches)* in next ch-7 sp and joining sl st, ch 5, **dtr-dc dec** *(see Special Stitches)* in same joining sl st and in next ch-7 sp, ch 7, sc in next ch-7 sp, ch 5, sc in next ch-7 sp, rep from * across, turn.

Row 2: Ch 3, sc in first ch-5 sp, *ch 5, hdc in next ch-7 sp, ch 3, (tr, ch 2, tr) in next ch-5 sp, ch 3, hdc in next ch-7 sp, ch 5, sc in next ch-5 sp, rep from * across.

Fasten off.

Finishing

Weave in end. Gently block if desired. ●

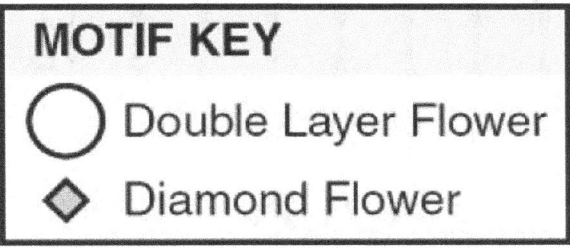

MOTIF KEY

◯ Double Layer Flower

◈ Diamond Flower

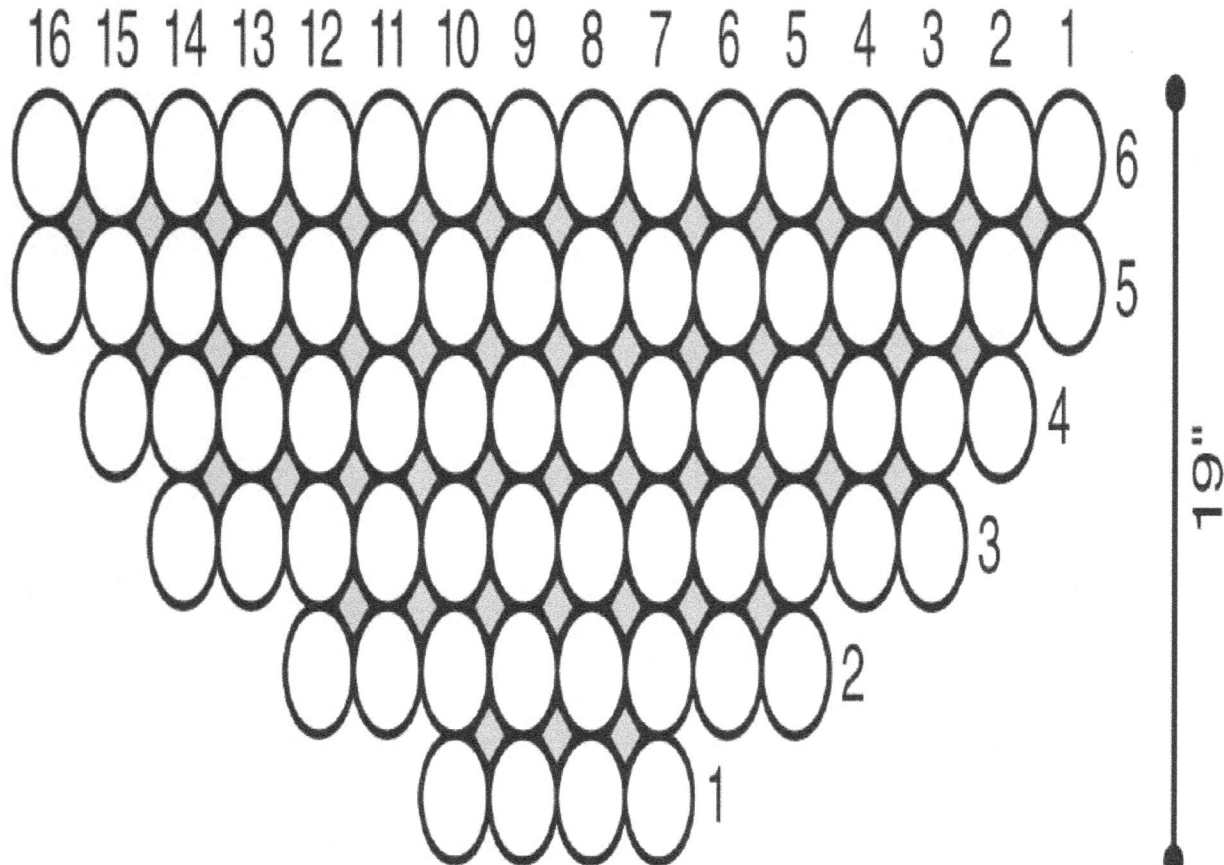

56"

19"

16 15 14 13 12 11 10 9 8 7 6 5 4 3 2 1

6

5

4

3

2

1

Petal Shawl
Assembly Diagram

Geometric Cowl

Skill Level

 **INTERMEDIATE**

Finished Measurements

6 inches wide x 25 inches in circumference

Materials

- Tahki Yarns Tandem medium (worsted) weight cotton/viscose/nylon/acrylic yarn (1¾ oz/107 yds/50g per hank):
  - 1 hank #06 northern lights

- Tahki Yarns Cotton Classic Lite fine (sport) weight cotton yarn (1¾ oz/146 yds/50g per hank):
  - 1 hank #4830 bright turquoise

FINE

- Aunt Lydia's Classic Crochet size 10 crochet cotton (350 yds per ball):
    1 ball #856 peacock

LACE

- Size F/5/3.75mm crochet hook or size needed to obtain gauge
- Tapestry needle
- Large square loom
- Loom base
- Permanent fabric adhesive

Gauge
Motif = 3 inches wide x 2½ inches long, without edging

Pattern Notes
Motifs are joined in 2 rows of 8 motifs each using a join-as-you-go method when working the Edging.

Use fabric adhesive to secure knots on back of Flowers.

Join with slip stitch as indicated unless otherwise stated.

Special Stitches
Single crochet join (sc join): Place slip knot on hook, insert hook in indicated st, yo and draw up a lp, yo and draw through both lps on hook.

Half double crochet join (hdc join): Place slip knot on hook, yo, insert hook in indicated st, yo and draw up a lp, yo and draw through all lps on hook.

Cowl

Make 16 Square & Circle Flowers referring to Flower Patterns article with northern lights for petals and turquoise for darning.

First Ring Edging

First Flower

Sc join *(see Special Stitches)* peacock in any corner petal, (ch 3, sc) in same petal, [ch 1, (sc, ch 1) in each petal across to next corner, (sc, ch 3, sc) in corner] twice, ch 1, (sc, ch 1) in each petal across to next corner, sc in corner petal, ch 3, turn, leaving rem side unworked.

2nd Flower

Holding current Flower and previous Flower with WS tog, sc in corner of current Flower, [sl st in ch-1 sp on previous Flower, sc in next petal on current Flower] across to next corner, (sc, ch 1, sl st in corner ch-3 sp on previous Flower, ch 1, sc) in corner on current Flower, (ch 1, sc) in each petal across to next corner, ch 1, (sc, ch 3, sc) in corner petal, (ch 1, sc) in each petal across to next corner, ch 1, sc in corner petal, ch 3, turn, leaving last side unworked.

3rd–7th Flowers

Work as for 2nd Flower.

8th Flower

Work as for 2nd Flower from * to *, ch 1, holding current Flower and First Flower with WS tog and taking care to not twist ring, (sc, ch 1, sl st in corner ch-3 sp on First Flower, ch 1, sc) in corner on current Flower, [sl st in ch-1 sp on First Flower, sc in next petal on current Flower] across to next corner, ch 1, (sc, ch 1, sl st in corner ch-3 sp on First Flower, ch 1, sc) in corner on current Flower, turn to work across unworked edges of all Flowers.

Bottom Edging

Working across unworked edge of piece, *(ch 1, sc) in each petal across to next corner, ch 1, sc in corner petal, ch 1, sl st in ch-3 sp between Flowers, ch 1, sc in corner petal on next Flower, rep from * around, ch 1, **join** (see Pattern Notes) in first sc. Fasten off.

2nd Ring Edging

First Flower

Sc join in any corner petal, (ch 3, sc) in same petal, (ch 1, sc) in each petal across to next corner petal, ch 1, sc in corner petal, sl st in 5th ch-1 sp on any Flower on First Ring, [sl st in next ch-1 sp on First Ring Flower, sc in next petal on current Flower] 3 times, ch 1, sl st in next sl st between First Ring Flowers, ch 1, [sc in next petal on current Flower, sl st in next ch-1 sp on First Ring Flower] 4 times, (sc, ch 1, sl st in next ch-1 sp on First Ring Flower, ch 1, sc) in next corner petal on current Flower, (ch 1, sc) in each petal on current Flower across to next corner, ch 1, sc in corner petal, ch 3, turn, leaving rem side unworked.

2nd Flower

Holding current Flower and previous Flower with WS tog, sc in any corner petal on current Flower, [sl st in next ch-1 sp on previous Flower, sc in next petal on current Flower] across to next corner petal, (sc, ch 1, sl st in corner sp on previous Flower, ch 1, sc) in corner petal on current Flower, [sl st in next ch-1 sp on First Ring Flower, sc in next petal on current Flower] 3 times, ch 1, sl st in sl st between next First Ring Flowers, ch 1, [sc in next petal on current Flower, sl st in next ch-1 sp on First Ring Flower] 4 times, (sc, ch 1, sl st in next ch-1 sp on First Ring Flower, ch 1, sc) in next corner petal on current Flower, (ch 1, sc) in each petal across to next corner, ch 1, sc in corner petal, ch 3, turn, leaving rem side unworked.

3rd–7th Flowers
Work as for 2nd Flower.

8th Flower
Work as for 2nd Flower from * to *, (sc, ch 1, sl st in joining sl st between First Flower on 2nd Ring and corresponding First Ring Flower, ch 1, sc) in next corner sp on current Flower, [sl st in next ch-1 sp on First Flower on 2nd Ring, sc in next petal on current Flower] across to next corner petal, (sc, ch 1, sl st in corner ch-3 sp on First Flower, ch 1, sc) in corner petal, turn to work along unworked edge of piece.

Bottom Edging
Work as for Bottom Edging on First Ring. Fasten off.

Border
Rnd 1: Hdc join *(see Special Stitches)* in any ch sp on outer edge of Cowl, hdc in each rem ch sp, sc and sl st around, join in first hdc. Fasten off.

Rep rnd 1 on opposite edge of Cowl. ●

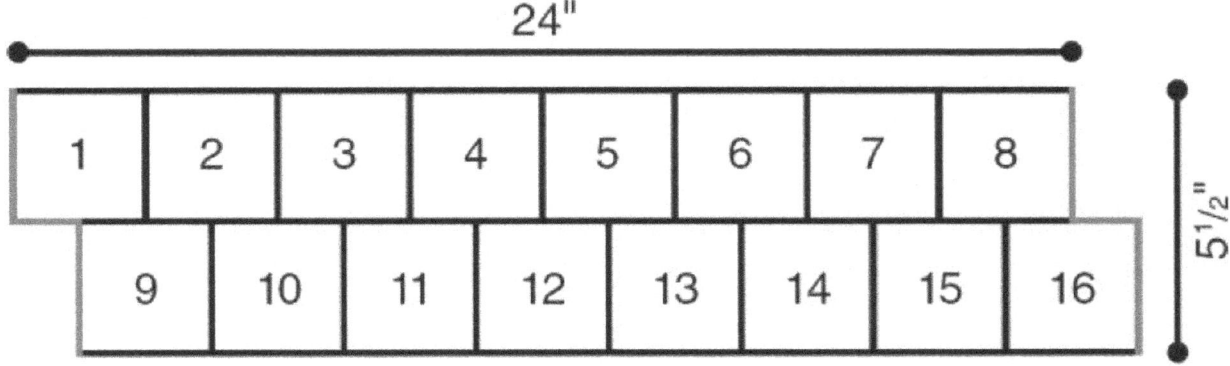

24"

| 1 | 2 | 3 | 4 | 5 | 6 | 7 | 8 |
| 9 | 10 | 11 | 12 | 13 | 14 | 15 | 16 |

5½"

Geometric Cowl
Assembly Diagram
Note: *Edges highlighted in red are joined to form piece into ring.*

Stunning Scarf

Skill Level

 INTERMEDIATE

Finished Measurements

6 inches wide x 60 inches long

Materials

- Patons Metallic medium (worsted) weight nylon/acrylic/wool yarn (3 oz/252 yds/85g per skein):
  1 skein each #5201 teal, # 5434 fuchsia and #5044 pewter

MEDIUM

- Plymouth Yarn Baby Alpaca Lace lace (lace) weight baby alpaca yarn (1¾ oz/437 yds/50g per hank):
  1 hank #2020 wine

LACE

- Size C/2/2.75mm crochet hook or size needed to obtain gauge
- Tapestry needle
- Large round loom
- Smallest round loom
- Loom base
- Permanent fabric adhesive

Gauge
14 chs = 2 inches

Pattern Notes
Use fabric adhesive to secure knots on back of Flowers.

Join with slip stitch as indicated unless otherwise stated.

A double petal is made from 2 loops on Double Layer Flower. Double Layer Flower has 12 double petals.

A long petal is 1 loop at corner on Diamond Flower. The remaining loops are petals. Diamond Flower has 4 long petals and 8 petals.

Special Stitches
Double crochet double treble crochet decrease (dc-dtr dec): Holding last lp of each st on hook, dc in indicated sp, **dtr** *(see Stitch Guide)* in next joining sl st, yo and draw through last 3 lps on hook.

Double treble crochet double crochet decrease (dtr-dc dec): Holding last lp of each st on hook, dtr in joining sl st, dc in indicated sp, yo and draw through last 3 lps on hook.

Single crochet join (sc join): Place slip knot on hook, insert hook in indicated st, yo and draw up a lp, yo and draw through both lps on hook.

Scarf

Make 38 Double Layer Flowers with teal outer petals, fuchsia inner petals and pewter for darning and 18 Diamond Flowers with pewter referring to Flower Patterns article.

First Row

First Double Layer Flower

Join *(see Pattern Notes)* wine in any **double petal** *(see Pattern Notes)*, [ch 7, sl st in next double petal] 4 times, ch 7, leave rem double petals unworked.

2nd Double Layer Flower

Sl st in any double petal of Next Flower, ch 3, sl st in ch-7 sp just made, ch 3, sl st in next double petal on same Flower, [ch 7, sl st in next double petal on same Flower] 5 times, ch 7, leave rem double petals unworked.

3rd–18th Double Layer Flowers

Work as for 2nd Double Layer Flower.

19th Double Layer Flower

Sl st in any double petal on Last Flower, ch 3, sl st in ch-7 sp just made, ch 3, sl st in next double petal on same Flower, [ch 7, sl st in next double petal on same Flower] 10 times, do not fasten off.

Bottom Edging

Now working across bottom of each Flower on First Row Edging, *ch 3, sl st in next ch-7 sp between Flowers, ch 3, sl st in double petal on next Flower, [ch 7, sl st in next double petal on same Flower] 4 times, rep from * across row to First Flower, ch 3, sl st in ch-7 sp between Flowers, ch 3, sl st in next double petal on First Flower, [ch 7, sl st in next double petal on same Flower] 6 times, ch 7, join in first sl st. Fasten off.

2nd Row

First Diamond Flower

Join wine in petal to right of any **long petal** *(see Pattern Notes)* on First Diamond Flower, ch 1, (sl st, ch 7, sl st) in next long petal, ch 1, sl st in next petal, ch 7, sl st in next petal, ch 1, (sl st, ch 3, sl st in 2nd ch-7 sp before join between Double Layer Flowers, ch 3, sl st) in next long petal, ch 1, sl st in next petal, ch 3, sl st in next ch-7 sp, ch 3, sl st in next petal, ch 1, (sl st, ch 3, sl st in joining sl st between next 2 Double Layer Flowers, ch 3, sl st) in next long petal, ch 1, sl st in next petal, ch 3, sl st in next ch-7 sp, ch 3, sl st in next petal, ch 1, (sl st, ch 3, sl st in next ch-7 sp, ch 3, sl st) in next long petal, ch 1, sl st in next petal, ch 7, join in first st. Fasten off.

2nd–18th Diamond Flowers

Work as for First Diamond Flower, working between Double Layer Flowers and using Assembly Diagram as a guide.

3rd Row

First Double Layer Flower

Join wine in any double petal, [ch 7, sl st in next double petal] 3 times, ch 3, sl st in ch-7 sp before joining sl st between adjacent Double Layer Flower and Diamond Flower, ch 3, sl st in next double petal, ch 3, sl st in joining sl st between adjacent Double Layer Flower and Diamond Flower, ch 3, sl st in next double petal, [ch 3, sl st in next ch-7 sp on adjacent Diamond Flower, ch 3, sl st in next double petal] twice, ch 7, do not fasten off.

2nd Double Layer Flower

*Sl st in any double petal, ch 3, sl st in joining sl st of previous Double Layer Flower and adjacent Diamond Flower, ch 3, sl st in next double petal, ch 3, sl st in next ch-7 sp on adjacent Diamond Flower, ch 3, sl st in next double petal, ch 3, sl st in next joining sl st between adjacent Diamond Flower and next Double Layer Flower, ch 3, sl st in next double petal**, ch 3, sl st in next joining sl st between adjacent Double Layer Flower and next Diamond Flower, ch 3, sl st in next double petal, [ch 3, sl st in next ch-7 sp on

Diamond Flower, ch 3, sl st in next double petal] twice, ch 7, do not fasten off. 7 double petals are joined on each adjacent Double Layer flower.

3rd–18th Double Layer

Flowers
Work as for 2nd Double Layer Flower.

19th Double Layer Flower
Work as for 2nd Double Layer Flower from * to **, ch 3, sl st in next ch-7 sp on adjacent Diamond Flower, ch 3, sl st in next double petal, [ch 7, sl st in next double petal] 7 times, do not fasten off.

Bottom Edging
Now working across bottom of each Flower on 2nd Row, *ch 3, sl st in ch-7 sp between first 2 Double

Layer Flowers, ch 3, sl st in next double petal, [ch 7, sl st in next double petal] 4 times, rep from * across, join in first sl st. Fasten off.

Long Edge Border

Row 1: With WS facing, **sc join** *(see Special Stitches)* wine in ch-7 sp at top of first Flower, ch 5, sc in next ch-7 sp, *ch 7, **dc-dtr dec** *(see Special Stitches)* in next ch-7 sp and joining sl st, ch 5, **dtr-dc dec** *(see Special Stitches)* in same joining sl st and in next ch-7 sp, ch 7, sc in next ch-7 sp, ch 5, sc in next ch-7 sp, rep from * across, turn.

Row 2: Ch 3, sc in first ch-5 sp, *ch 5, hdc in next ch-7 sp, ch 3, (tr, ch 2, tr) in next ch-5 sp, ch 3, hdc in next ch-7 sp, ch 5, sc in next ch-5 sp, rep from * across.

Fasten off.

Rep for opposite long edge.

Short Edge Border

Row 1: With WS facing, sc join wine in ch-7 sp at top of first flower, ch 5, sc in next ch-7 sp, ch 7, dc-dtr dec in next ch-7 sp and joining sl st, ch 5, dtr-dc dec in same joining sl st and in next ch-7 sp, ch 7, sc in next ch-7 sp, ch 5, sc in next ch-7 sp, turn.

Row 2: Ch 3, sc in first ch-5 sp, *ch 5, hdc in next ch-7 sp, ch 3, (tr, ch 2, tr) in next ch-5 sp, ch 3, hdc in next ch-7 sp, ch 5, sc in next ch-5 sp.

Fasten off.

Rep for opposite short edge.

Finishing

Weave in end. Gently block if desired.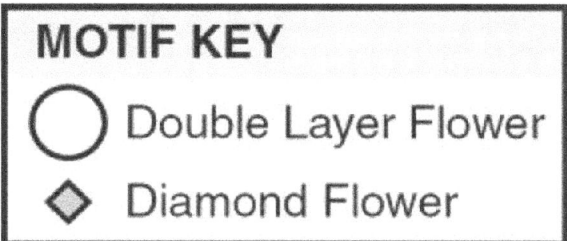

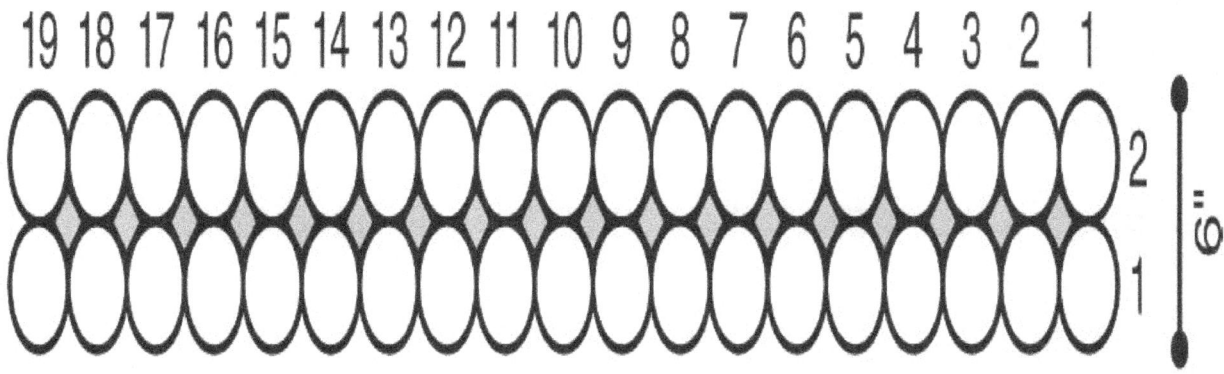

Stunning Scarf

Assembly Diagram

STITCH ABBREVIATIONS

beg	begin/begins/beginning
bpdc	back post double crochet
bpsc	back post single crochet
bptr	back post treble crochet
CC	contrasting color
ch(s)	chain(s)
ch-	refers to chain or space previously made (i.e., ch-1 space)
ch sp(s)	chain space(s)
cl(s)	cluster(s)
cm	centimeter(s)
dc	double crochet (singular/plural)
dc dec	double crochet 2 or more stitches together, as indicated
dec	decrease/decreases/decreasing
dtr	double treble crochet
ext	extended
fpdc	front post double crochet
fpsc	front post single crochet
fptr	front post treble crochet
g	gram(s)
hdc	half double crochet
hdc dec	half double crochet 2 or more stitches together, as indicated
inc	increase/increases/increasing

lp(s)	loop(s)
MC	main color
mm	millimeter(s)
oz	ounce(s)
pc	popcorn(s)
rem	remain/remains/remaining
rep(s)	repeat(s)
rnd(s)	round(s)
RS	right side
sc	single crochet (singular/plural)
sc dec	single crochet 2 or more stitches together, as indicated
sk	skip/skipped/skipping
sl st(s)	slip stitch(es)
sp(s)	space(s)/spaced
st(s)	stitch(es)
tog	together
tr	treble crochet
trtr	triple treble
WS	wrong side
yd(s)	yard(s)
yo	yarn over

YARN CONVERSION
OUNCES TO GRAMS

1	28.4
2	56.7
3	85.0
4	113.4

GRAMS TO OUNCES

25	⅞

40	1⅔
50	1¾
100	3½

UNITED STATES		UNITED KINGDOM
sl st (slip stitch)	=	sc (single crochet)
sc (single crochet)	=	dc (double crochet)
hdc (half double crochet)	=	htr (half treble crochet)
dc (double crochet)	=	tr (treble crochet)
tr (treble crochet)	=	dtr (double treble crochet)
dtr (double treble crochet)	=	ttr (triple treble crochet)
skip	=	miss

Single crochet decrease (sc dec):

(Insert hook, yo, draw lp through) in each of the sts indicated, yo, draw through all lps on hook.

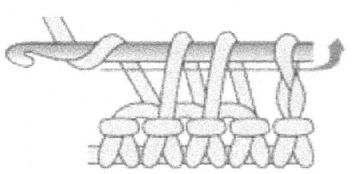

Example of 2-sc dec

Half double crochet decrease (hdc dec):

(Yo, insert hook, yo, draw lp through) in each of the sts indicated, yo, draw through all lps on hook.

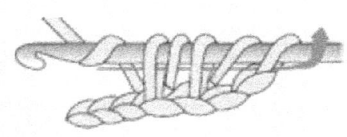

Example of 2-hdc dec

Reverse single crochet (reverse sc): Ch 1, sk first st, working from left to right, insert hook in next st from front to back, draw up lp on hook, yo and draw through both lps on hook.

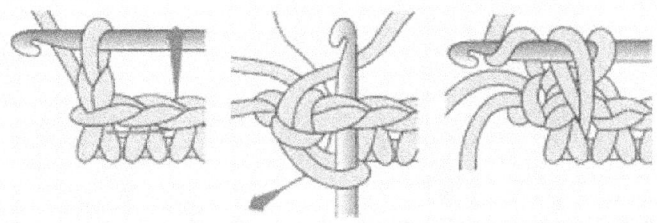

Chain (ch): Yo, pull through lp on hook.

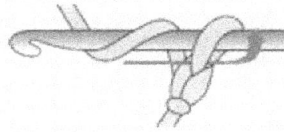

Single crochet (sc): Insert hook in st, yo, pull through st, yo, pull through both lps on hook.

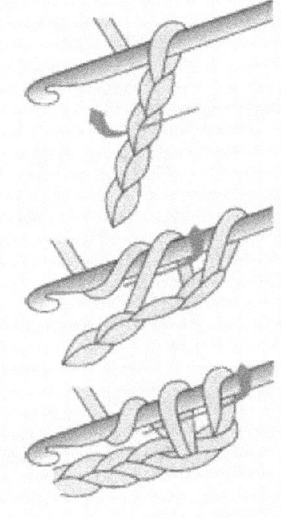

Double crochet (dc): Yo, insert hook in st, yo, pull through st, [yo, pull through 2 lps] twice.

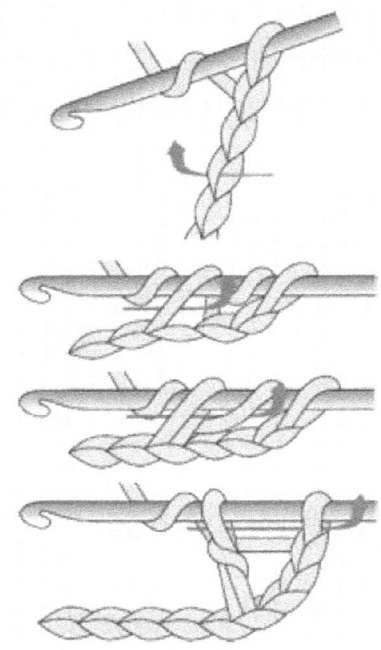

Double crochet decrease (dc dec): (Yo, insert hook, yo, draw lp through, yo, draw through 2 lps on hook) in each of the sts indicated, yo, draw through all lps on hook.

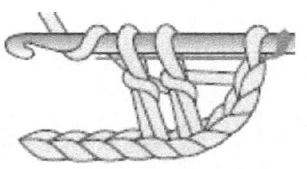

Example of 2-dc dec

Front loop (front lp) Back loop (back lp)

Front Loop   Back Loop

Front post stitch (fp): Back post stitch (bp):
When working post st, insert hook from right to left around post of st on previous row.

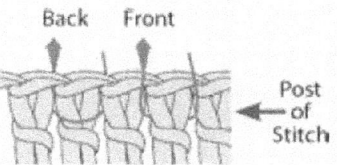

Half double crochet (hdc): Yo, insert hook in st, yo, pull through st, yo, pull through all 3 lps on hook.

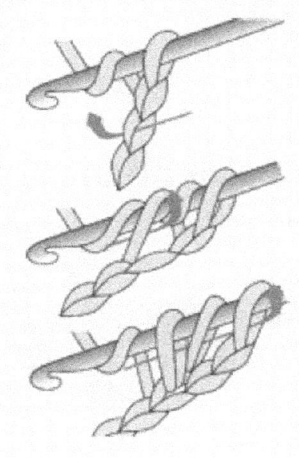

Double treble crochet (dtr): Yo 3 times, insert hook in st, yo, pull through st, [yo, pull through 2 lps] 4 times.

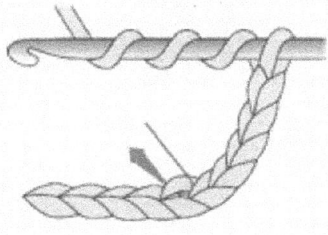

Treble crochet decrease (tr dec): Holding back last lp of each st, tr in each of the sts indicated, yo, pull through all lps on hook.

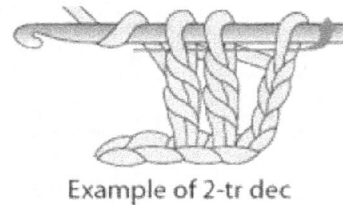

Example of 2-tr dec

Slip stitch (sl st): Insert hook in st, pull through both lps on hook.

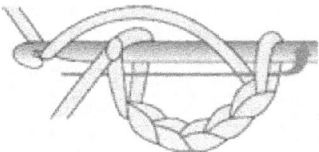

Chain color change (ch color change) Yo with new color, draw through last lp on hook.

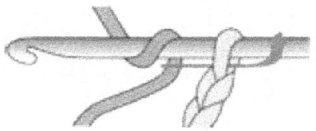

Double crochet color change (dc color change) Drop first color, yo with new color, draw through last 2 lps of st.

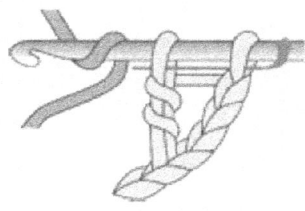

Treble crochet (tr): Yo twice, insert hook in st, yo, pull through st, [yo, pull through 2 lps] 3 times.

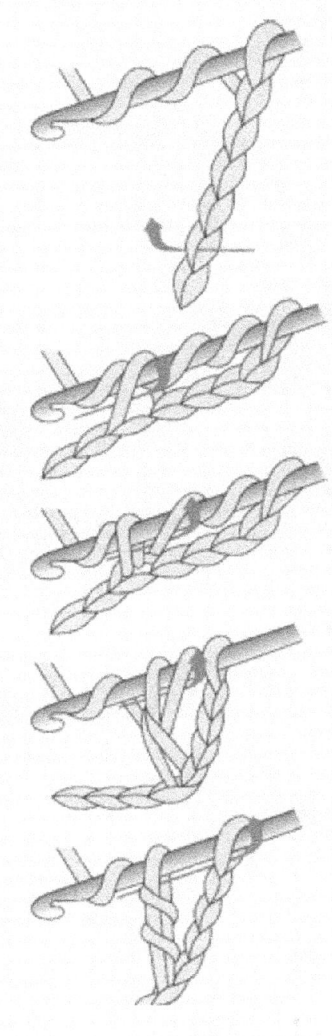

Metric Conversion Charts

METRIC CONVERSIONS

yards	x	.9144	=	metres (m)
yards	x	91.44	=	centimetres (cm)
inches	x	2.54	=	centimetres (cm)
inches	x	25.40	=	millimetres (mm)
inches	x	.0254	=	metres (m)

centimetres	x	.3937	=	inches
metres	x	1.0936	=	yards

INCHES INTO MILLIMETRES & CENTIMETRES (Rounded off slightly)

inches	mm	cm	inches	cm	inches	cm	inches	cm
1/8	3	0.3	5	12.5	21	53.5	38	96.5
1/4	6	0.6	5 1/2	14	22	56	39	99
3/8	10	1	6	15	23	58.5	40	101.5
1/2	13	1.3	7	18	24	61	41	104
5/8	15	1.5	8	20.5	25	63.5	42	106.5
3/4	20	2	9	23	26	66	43	109
7/8	22	2.2	10	25.5	27	68.5	44	112
1	25	2.5	11	28	28	71	45	114.5
1 1/4	32	3.2	12	30.5	29	73.5	46	117
1 1/2	38	3.8	13	33	30	76	47	119.5
1 3/4	45	4.5	14	35.5	31	79	48	122
2	50	5	15	38	32	81.5	49	124.5
2 1/2	65	6.5	16	40.5	33	84	50	127
3	75	7.5	17	43	34	86.5		
3 1/2	90	9	18	46	35	89		
4	100	10	19	48.5	36	91.5		
4 1/2	115	11.5	20	51	37	94		

KNITTING NEEDLES CONVERSION CHART

Canada/U.S.	0	1	2	3	4	5	6	7	8	9	10	10½	11	13	15
Metric (mm)	2	2¼	2¾	3¼	3½	3¾	4	4½	5	5½	6	6½	8	9	10

CROCHET HOOKS CONVERSION CHART

Canada/U.S.	1/B	2/C	3/D	4/E	5/F	6/G	8/H	9/I	10/J	10½/K	N
Metric (mm)	2.25	2.75	3.25	3.5	3.75	4.25	5	5.5	6	6.5	9.0